*Collector's Library*

# LOVE POETRY

# LOVE POETRY

*Edited and with an Introduction by*
JULIETTE MITCHELL

*Collector's Library*

This edition published in 2014 by
*Collector's Library*
an imprint of CRW Publishing Limited
69 Gloucester Crescent, London NW1 7EG

ISBN 978 1 909621 10 7

Introduction and Text copyright ©
CRW Publishing Limited 2014

Typeset in Great Britain by Antony Gray
Printed and bound in China by Imago

1

# Contents

# Introduction

Love and poetry – what a perfect match! There's
nothing quite like an anthology of love poetry to
remind one of the power of words or, for that matter,
the power of love. Prose might do the job of telling a
love story from beginning to end, from the first
encounter with one's beloved to the 'happily ever
after', but if it's a case of putting into words the
strength, the depth and the intensity of an emotion –
and, in the end, what is love but one of the strongest,
most world-shattering emotions? – then we need
something stronger. We need poetry.

But what is it about poetry which gives it this extra
kick and makes it so well suited to expressing our
deepest feelings? For a start, there's nothing
haphazard about a poem. Each word is chosen not
just for its meaning and whatever associations that
meaning might set off within us, but for every other
aspect of its being: its sound, its rhythm and the way
it sits on the page. In short, the word becomes
something almost physical. And then there's the way
the words spark off each other, shifting, bending,
altering as they do so. The whole thing is a kind of
dance in which the words are part of an intricate,
moving formation. And what of the person behind
this dance of words? The poet is not some
disinterested choreographer calling from the sidelines
but a thinking, feeling human being fully invested in
the process. We know that writers – even those who
might at other times be novelists or playwrights or

even critics – turn to poetry when the experience of life calls for nothing less than the most intense form of expression. A poem is a short, sharp burst of emotion; a way of getting straight to the point; a cry from the depths of the heart.

Of course, even for the non-poets among us, one of the side-effects of love is that we feel the need to express it, and sometimes a simple 'I love you' can't quite reach to the edges of what we're trying to express. A poet writing about love is a poet in thrall to his craft and thankful for the relief that putting love into words brings. Poetry, in other words, is a happy meeting of expression and emotion – and a kind of short cut for both. So while a novelist might delve into a character's state of mind over the expanse of a hundred pages, a poet's preoccupation is with grasping it fully and quickly, and wrapping it up in just a handful of stanzas (and sometimes less). If words on the page can ever claim to be three-dimensional, then, we're more likely to find those words in poetry than in any other form.

But for all their physicality and the confident mark they make on the page, there is something fragile and intimate about many of the poems that follow. 'Tread softly because you tread on my dreams,' says W. B. Yeats, hinting at the vulnerability we all possess when we succumb to our emotions and lay them bare. And, in fact, it is difficult to do anything but tread softly as we read the poems here. There is love of all kinds – requited, unrequited, spurned, blissful, platonic, lost – but, whatever the hue of the love expressed, the poet appeals to our humanity. Reading a love poem is not simply a case of hearing a distant song; instead, it's a chance to hear our own heartbeat slightly more clearly. For, when poetry succeeds, it brings us just a little closer to an understanding of our own experience, our own feelings, our own dreams.

And, whatever our state of mind when we turn to a love poem, we are inviting another's experience into these dreams of ours. In other words, we need to tread softly for our own sakes, too. We may simply be enjoying the beauty of the emotions coupled with the beauty of the words, or we may be reading 'to know we are not alone' (as C. S. Lewis said), or we may be reading to better understand what we ourselves are living through; but as we know – and whatever our motive – poetry can cut to the quick, and it can take us out of our own experience into someone else's and back into our own far more powerfully than we expect. And the same poem, on a different day, can affect us in a different way. Even for the least invested among us, it's emotional terrain.

Poetry can be like the best kind of conversation, then: a heart-to-heart which leaves the readers feeling a little more understood and a little more themselves. And, for those of us looking for solace, poetry offers another possibility. The kind of predicament that might seem too painful for words when we ourselves are going through it, may – in the words of a poet – be delivered with a lightness of touch which elevates the most dismal suffering into something beautiful. Poetry heightens experience (the dark might become darker still) but at the same time makes it palatable. In other words, the unbearable becomes bearable. Poets, it turns out, can give us words to guide us through the most difficult times.

But poetry is another kind of conversation too, and by allowing the poets to follow one another in chronological order – by date of death rather than date of birth, since most poets are obviously more productive in their later years than their early ones – we can sense more clearly the way they talk to each other across the years and centuries. So the themes developed by one and picked up by another, the idiom handed down from one century to the next, one poet's concerns chiming with the concerns of another – these are the kind of things that we hope your ear will be alive to as you read. We trust you'll enjoy reading and discovering each poet in the context of their time and alongside their contemporaries, as well as feeling the way poetry has evolved over the centuries, with one poet's successor being another poet's predecessor.

Some centuries are, of course, better represented here than others. We begin with a few translations of ancient poetry to set the scene and remind us of the timelessness of love, and there's then a rather prolonged silence, with just the brief appearance of a few lines from Edward Fitzgerald's translation of the *Rubáiyát of Omar Khayyám*, before Chaucer eventually emerges: England before Chaucer – at least in the way it manifested itself in poetry – was a harsh, masculine world and spoke more of the battlefield than it did of love. But with Chaucer love came to the fore, in a language which would be taken up and developed by his literary heirs. But there was still something missing, and for love poetry truly to flourish in England a new mindset was needed, and it wasn't until the sixteenth century that the stage was finally set. By this time the influence of the Italian Renaissance had spread northwards and changed the cultural landscape for ever, and a whole host of poets began to write in a language – and with a sensibility – that we can easily take pleasure in today: Christopher Marlowe, William Shakespeare, Edmund Spenser, Thomas More, Sir Philip Sidney and John Milton. Classicism and the court were still their major points of reference, but love – however idealised and chivalrous – had become a popular theme.

Love has remained a preoccupation among poets ever since, but the shifts in language and approach over the next few centuries were considerable. The seventeenth century saw the Metaphysical poets – John Donne, Andrew Marvell, George Herbert and others – deepening their gaze and thinking more searchingly about the subject; love was most definitely a concern for philosophical and religious exploration. And these poets introduced a new wit and ironic tone into much of what they wrote. Meanwhile, the Cavalier poets – Ben Jonson and Robert Herrick, for example – were being being influenced and shaped by the tastes of Charles I and his court, and their poems were lighthearted, lively and celebrated love in its more superficial manifestations.

Of course telling the story of poetry so neatly would be impossible without the benefit of hindsight, but the way that literature was shaped by political and social movements – and especially by royalty – during the seventeenth and eighteenth centuries does mean that a relatively clear poetic path is visible. And the Restoration of the English monarchy in 1660 brought with it a new sophistication as well as the kind of immorality and rakishness we see in John Wilmot, Earl of Rochester. From here it was an easy progression to the satire, scepticism and return to classical forms of the eighteenth century. This was the Age of Enlightenment, and love was not high on the agenda.

But now, with the end of the eighteenth century just round the corner, England was ripe for the Romantic movement. Poets reacted against the beginnings of industrialisation and the tenets of the Enlightenment – reason and the individual will – and turned instead to intuition and emotion as driving forces. They began to focus increasingly on their own feelings and the need to express themselves. So we have William Blake, William Wordsworth, Samuel Taylor Coleridge, Percy Bysshe Shelley, Lord Byron and John Keats elevating love to the status of a subject eminently worthy of poetry. And these Romantics – and particularly William Wordsworth – paved the way for the poets of the Victorian age.

The nineteenth century was, of course, a time of significant social change, of the rise of the New World, and of increasing industrialisation. Women poets were now coming to the fore (Elizabeth Barrett Browning, Christina Rossetti and Emily Dickinson are fine examples), and poets from America were making a name for themselves (Walt Whitman, Ralph Waldo Emerson and, again, Emily Dickinson). But, in essence, poetry still shared the sensibility of the Romantics, and self-expression – along with a healthy dose of religious scepticism and the odd bit of light relief – was still paramount. Love, not surprisingly, features in the work of many of the nineteenth century's greatest poets.

And now we are on the cusp of the twentieth century, and a new sensibility is starting to develop. Poets are ready to break from traditional forms, and the cultural landscape is in need of new points of reference. Thomas Hardy, W. B. Yeats and A. E. Housman – while still talking, among other things, of love – are ushering in a new way of looking at things and using a new, crisper language to express what they see. Soon the old century is behind them, and the twentieth century has brought with it a new movement: modernism.

But standing back and making out the shape of cultural movements is but one way of appreciating poetry, and we hope this whistle-stop tour through poetic developments won't stop you focusing on the words themselves. A good poem can stand alone and speak for itself – and it certainly doesn't need any kind of explanation to prop it up. So the poems you'll find here have the strength to speak across the centuries, and their rhythms, sounds and meanings still ring loud and clear. They have stood the test of time and are all, in their own way, classics.

Once we alight on a poem, we may choose to read it to ourselves, intoned under our breath or out loud. And, if aloud, it may be so that we, and we alone, may hear its sounds more clearly. Or we may perhaps be sharing its pleasures with the object of our affections. Or – a very different scenario – we may be calling upon poetry's more public face at a wedding or other special occasion; sometimes what we're looking for is a way of talking about the depth of our feelings without exposing those feelings themselves. In these cases, the words of another might be exactly what we're looking for, and the rhythmic pace of a well-crafted love poem, with its formal livery and beautiful cadences, make poetry the perfect form for expressing our love to an audience. Poetry gives us a socially acceptable, very presentable language of love with which to touch on things we might not normally share. So whether we need Kahlil Gibran to give advice on how best to let love flourish or Shakespeare to make a far-fetched – but perfect – comparison, we can find a poem to convey what we would say if only we had the words, and if only we had the courage.

Perhaps these kinds of public occasions are the times when poems really show their timelessness, their true colours and their relevance to our own lives. In any case, we hope you'll find plenty of poems here that speak directly to you, even in your more private moments. There'll be poems which are at once pleasantly familiar, poems you might have studied in the classroom and still half-remember, and other notable and beautiful poems which you wish you had come across before. And if you find just one favourite poem somewhere between these covers, then this book will have earned its keep and justified the sliver of space it takes up on your shelf. But our hope is that you will find many favourites here, and that this collection will earn its place many times over. We hope it will loiter by your bed and accompany you on your travels. For there's something about the very best of poems, about the spring in their step and the power of their words, which means they should always be close at hand for you to turn to whenever the mood takes you – and wherever life takes you.

JULIETTE MITCHELL

Juliette Mitchell is a writer, editor and teacher. She lives in Lewes, East Sussex.

*Love Poetry*

## Further Reading

Terry Eagleton, *How to Read a Poem*, Blackwell, 2007

James Fenton, *An Introduction to English Poetry*, Penguin, 2003

Margaret Ferguson, Mary Jo Salter and Jon Stallworthy (eds), *The Norton Anthology of Poetry*, W. W. Norton, 2005

Anthony Low, *The Reinvention of Love: Poetry, Politics and Culture from Sidney to Milton*, Cambridge University Press, 2008

Phil Roberts, *How Poetry Works*, Penguin, 2000

Pat Rogers (ed.), *The Oxford Illustrated History of English Literature*, Oxford, 2001

Jeffrey Wainwright, *Poetry: The Basics*, Routledge, 2011

# LOVE POETRY

# SAPPHO

### *Translated by*
### DANTE GABRIEL ROSSETTI

## *One Girl*

I

Like the sweet apple which reddens upon the
                              topmost bough,
Atop on the topmost twig, – which the pluckers
                              forgot, somehow, –
Forget it not, nay; but got it not, for none could
                              get it till now.

2

Like the wild hyacinth flower which on the hills
                              is found,
Which the passing feet of the shepherds for ever
                              tear and wound,
Until the purple blossom is trodden in the ground.

*Translated and adapted by*
THOMAS CAMPION

*(Catullus 5)*

## My Sweetest Lesbia

My sweetest Lesbia, let us live and love,
And, though the sager sort our deeds reprove,
Let us not weigh them: heaven's great lamps do dive
Into their west, and straight again revive,
But, soon as once set is our little light,
Then must we sleep one ever-during night.

If all would lead their lives in love like me,
Then bloody swords and armour should not be,
No drum nor trumpet peaceful sleeps should move,
Unless alarm came from the camp of love:
But fools do live, and waste their little light,
And seek with pain their ever-during night.

When timely death my life and fortune ends,
Let not my hearse be vexed with mourning friends,
But let all lovers, rich in triumph come,
And with sweet pastimes grace my happy tomb;
And, Lesbia, close up thou my little light,
And crown with love my ever-during night.

## HORACE

*Translated by*
Abraham Cowley

*(from 'Odes', Book 3, 15)*

## *Love and Gold*

### I

A Tower of Brass, one would have said,
And Locks, and Bolts, and Iron Bars,
Might have preserv'd one innocent Maidenhead.
The jealous Father thought he well might spare
All further jealous Care.
And, as he walk'd, t'himself alone he smiled,
To think how Venus' Arts he had beguil'd;
    And when he slept, his Rest was deep:
    But Venus laugh'd, to see and hear him sleep:
        She taught the am'rous Jove
        A magical Receipt in Love,
Which arm'd him stronger, and which help'd
                                him more,
Than all his Thunder did, and his Almightyship
                            before.

### 2

She taught him Love's Elixir, by which Art
His Godhead into Gold he did convert;
    No Guards did then his Passage stay,
    He pass'd with Ease, Gold was the Word;
Subtle as Light'ning, bright, and quick, and fierce,
Gold thro' Doors and Walls did pierce;
And as that works sometimes upon the Sword,

Melted the Maidenhead away,
Ev'n in the secret Scabbard where it lay.
The prudent Macedonian King,
To blow up Towns a Golden Mine did spring;
He broke thro' Gates with this Petarr,
'Tis the great Art of Peace, the Engine 'tis of War;
And Fleets and Armies follow it afar;
The Ensign 'tis at Land: and 'tis the Seaman's Star.

OVID

*Translated and adapted by*
CHRISTOPHER MARLOWE
*(Book One, 5)*

## Elegies

In summer's heat and mid-time of the day
To rest my limbs upon a bed I lay,
One window shut, the other open stood,
Which gave such light as twinkles in a wood,
Like twilight glimpse at setting of the sun
Or night being past, and yet not day begun.
Such light to shamefaced maidens must be shown,
Where they may sport, and seem to be unknown.
Then came Corinna in a long loose gown,
Her white neck hid with tresses hanging down:
Resembling fair Semiramis going to bed
Or Laïs of a thousand wooers sped.
I snatched her gown, being thin, the harm was small,
Yet strived she to be covered therewithal.
And striving thus as one that would be cast,
Betrayed herself, and yielded at the last.
Stark naked as she stood before mine eye,
Not one wen in her body could I spy.

What arms and shoulders did I touch and see,
How apt her breasts were to be pressed by me?
How smooth a belly under her waist saw I?
How large a leg, and what a lusty thigh?
To leave the rest, all liked me passing well,
I clinged her naked body, down she fell,
Judge you the rest: being tired she bad me kiss,
Jove send me more such afternoons as this.

PETRONIUS

*Translated by*
BEN JONSON

## Doing, a Filthy Pleasure is, and Short

Doing, a filthy pleasure is, and short;
And done, we straight repent us of the sport:
Let us not then rush blindly on unto it,
Like lustful beasts, that only know to do it:
For lust will languish, and that heat decay.
But thus, thus, keeping endless holiday,
Let us together closely lie and kiss,
There is no labour, nor no shame in this;
This hath pleased, doth please, and long
                    will please; never
Can this decay, but is beginning ever.

OMAR KHAYYÁM

*Translated and adapted by*
EDWARD FITZGERALD

FROM *The Rubáiyát of Omar Khayyám*

Here with a Loaf of Bread beneath the Bough,
A Flask of Wine, a Book of Verse – and Thou
    Beside me singing in the Wilderness –
And Wilderness is Paradise enow.

## FROM *Rondel of Merciless Beauty*

Your eyen two wol slee me sodenly,
I may the beautè of hem not sustene,
So woundeth hit throughout my herte kene

And but your word wol helen hastily
My hertes wounde, whyl that hit is grene,
Your eyen two wol slee me sodenly,
I may the beautè of hem not sustene.

Upon my trouthe I sey yow feithfully,
That ye ben of my lyf and deeth the quene;
For with my deeth the trouthe shal be sene.
Your eyen two wol slee me sodenly,
I may the beautè of hem not sustene,
So woundeth hit throughout my herte kene.

## GEOFFREY CHAUCER

### *The Love Unfeigned*

O yonge fresshe folkes, he or she,
In which that love up groweth with your age,
Repeyreth hoom from worldly vanitee,
And of your herte up-casteth the visage
To thilke god that after his image
Yow made, and thinketh al nis but a fayre
This world, that passeth sone as floures fayre.

And loveth him, the which that right for love
Upon a cros, our soules for to beye,
First starf, and roos, and sit in hevene above;
For he nil falsen no wight, dar I seye,
That wol his herte al hoolly on him leye.
And sin he best to love is, and most meke,
What nedeth feyned loves for to seke?

### ANONYMOUS
#### (*Early Sixteenth Century*)

### *Westron Wynde*

Westron wynde, when will thou blow
The small rain down can rain
Christ, that my love were in my arms
And I in my bed again

SIR PHILIP SIDNEY

(*Sonnet 1*)

## *Loving in Truth*

Loving in truth, and fain in verse my love to show,
That the dear She might take some pleasure of
                                    my pain,
Pleasure might cause her read, reading might
                                    make her know,
Knowledge might pity win, and pity grace obtain,
I sought fit words to paint the blackest face of woe,
Studying inventions fine, her wits to entertain:
Oft turning others' leaves, to see if thence would flow
Some fresh and fruitful showers upon my sun-
                                    burned brain.
But words came halting forth, wanting Invention's stay,
Invention, Nature's child, fled step-dame
                                    Study's blows,
And others' feet still seemed but strangers in my way.
Thus great with child to speak, and helpless
                                    in my throes,
Biting my truant pen, beating myself for spite:
'Fool,' said my Muse to me, look in thy heart and write.

# SIR PHILIP SIDNEY

*(Sonnet 31)*

## *With How Sad Steps*

With how sad steps, O moon, thou climb'st the skies!
How silently, and with how wan a face!
What! may it be that even in heavenly place
That busy archer his sharp arrows tries?
Sure, if that long-with-love-acquainted eyes
Can judge of love, thou feel'st a lover's case:
I read it in thy looks; thy languished grace
To me, that feel the like, thy state descries.
Then, even of fellowship, O Moon, tell me,
Is constant love deemed there but want of wit?
Are beauties there as proud as here they be?
Do they above love to be loved, and yet
    Those lovers scorn whom that love doth possess?
    Do they call 'virtue' there – ungratefulness?

SIR PHILIP SIDNEY

## My True Love Hath My Heart

My true love hath my heart and I have his,
By just exchange one for the other given:
I hold his dear, and mine he cannot miss;
There never was a bargain better driven.
His heart in me keeps me and him in one;
My heart in him his thoughts and senses guides:
He loves my heart, for once it was his own;
I cherish his because in me it bides.
His heart his wound received from my sight;
My heart was wounded with his wounded heart;
For as from me on him his hurt did light,
So still, methought, in me his hurt did smart:
Both equal hurt, in this change sought our bliss,
My true love hath my heart and I have his.


SIR PHILIP SIDNEY

## When, to My Deadly Pleasure

When, to my deadly pleasure,
When to my lively torment,
Lady, mine eyes remained
Joined, alas, to your beams.

With violence of heavenly
Beauty, tied to virtue;
Reason abashed retired;
Gladly my senses yielded.

Gladly my senses yielding,
Thus to betray my heart's fort,
Left me devoid of all life.

They to the beamy suns went,
Where, by the death of all deaths,
Find to what harm they hastened.

Like to the silly Sylvan,
Burned by the light he best liked,
When with a fire he first met.

Yet, yet, a life to their death,
Lady you have reserved;
Lady the life of all love.

For though my sense be from me,
And I be dead, who want sense,
Yet do we both live in you.

Turned anew, by your means,
Unto the flower that aye turns,
As you, alas, my sun bends.

Thus do I fall to rise thus;
Thus do I die to live thus;
Changed to a change, I change not.

Thus may I not be from you;
Thus be my senses on you;
Thus what I think is of you;
Thus what I seek is in you;
    All what I am, it is you.

*Love Poetry*

CHRISTOPHER MARLOWE

## *The Passionate Shepherd to His Love*

Come live with me and be my love,
And we will all the pleasures prove,
That Valleys, groves, hills, and fields,
Woods, or steepy mountain yields.

And we will sit upon the Rocks,
Seeing the Shepherds feed their flocks,
By shallow Rivers to whose falls
Melodious birds sing Madrigals.

And I will make thee beds of Roses
And a thousand fragrant posies,
A cap of flowers, and a kirtle
Embroidered all with leaves of Myrtle;

A gown made of the finest wool
Which from our pretty Lambs we pull;
Fair lined slippers for the cold,
With buckles of the purest gold;

A belt of straw and Ivy buds,
With Coral clasps and Amber studs:
And if these pleasures may thee move,
Come live with me, and be my love.

The Shepherds' Swains shall dance and sing
For thy delight each May-morning:
If these delights thy mind may move,
Then live with me, and be my love.

CHRISTOPHER MARLOWE

## *Who Ever Loved that Loved Not at First Sight?*

It lies not in our power to love or hate,
For will in us is overruled by fate.
When two are stripped, long ere the course begin,
We wish that one should love, the other win;

And one especially do we affect
Of two gold ingots, like in each respect:
The reason no man knows; let it suffice
What we behold is censured by our eyes.
Where both deliberate, the love is slight:
Who ever loved, that loved not at first sight?

*Love Poetry*

CHRISTOPHER MARLOWE

# The Face That Launched a Thousand Ships

*from* DOCTOR FAUSTUS

Was this the face that launched a thousand ships,
And burnt the topless towers of Ilium?
Sweet Helen, make me immortal with a kiss.
Her lips suck forth my soul, see where it flies!
Come, Helen, come, give me my soul again.
Here will I dwell, for heaven is in these lips,
And all is dross that is not Helena.
I will be Paris, and for love of thee,
Instead of Troy, shall Wittenberg be sacked;
And I will combat with weak Menelaus,
And wear thy colours on my plumed crest;
Yea, I will wound Achilles in the heel,
And then return to Helen for a kiss.
O, thou art fairer than the evening air
Clad in the beauty of a thousand stars;
Brighter art thou than flaming Jupiter
When he appeared to hapless Semele;
More lovely than the monarch of the sky
In wanton Arethusa's azured arms;
And none but thou shalt be my paramour!

(*Sonnet 75*)

## *Amoretti*

One day I wrote her name upon the strand,
　But came the waves and washed it away:
Again I wrote it with a second hand,
　But came the tide, and made my pains his prey.
'Vain man,' said she, 'that dost in vain assay,
　A mortal thing so to immortalise;
For I myself shall like to this decay,
　And eek my name be wiped out likewise.'
'Not so,' quoth I, 'let baser things devise
　To die in dust, but you shall live by fame:
My verse your virtues rare shall eternise,
　And in the heavens write your glorious name:
Where whenas death shall all the world subdue,
Our love shall live, and later life renew.'

EDMUND SPENSER

## *Iambicum Trimetrum*

Unhappy verse, the witness of my unhappy state,
  Make thy self fluttering wings of thy fast flying
  Thought, and fly forth unto my love, wheresoever
                                she be:
Whether lying restless in heavy bed, or else
  Sitting so cheerless at the cheerful board, or else
  Playing alone careless on her heavenly virginals.
If in bed, tell her that my eyes can take no rest;
  If at board, tell her that my mouth can eat no meat;
  If at her virginals, tell her I can hear no mirth.
Asked why? say: waking love suffereth no sleep;
  Say that raging love doth appal the weak stomach;
  Say that lamenting love marreth the musical.
Tell her that her pleasures were wont to lull
                             me asleep;
  Tell her that her beauty was wont to feed
                             mine eyes;
  Tell her that her sweet tongue was wont to
                           make me mirth.
Now do I nightly waste, wanting my kindly rest;
  Now do I daily starve, wanting my lively food;
  Now do I always die, wanting thy timely mirth.
And if I waste, who will bewail my heavy chance?
  And if I starve, who will record my cursed end?
  And if I die, who will say, *this was Immerito*?

## A Silent Love

The lowest trees have tops, the ant her gall,
The fly her spleen, the little sparks their heat;
The slender hairs cast shadows, though but small,
And bees have stings, although they be not great;
    Seas have their source, and so have shallow springs;
    And love is love, in beggars as in kings.

Where waters smoothest run, there deepest are
                      the fords;
The dial stirs, yet none perceives it move;
The firmest faith is in the fewest words;
The turtles cannot sing, and yet they love:
    True hearts have eyes and ears, no tongues to speak;
    They hear and see, and sigh, and then they break.

## SIR JOHN HARINGTON

### *The Author to his Wife, of a Woman's Eloquence*

My Mall, I mark that when you mean to prove me
To buy a velvet gown, or some rich border,
Thou call'st me good sweet heart, thou swear'st
                    to love me,
Thy locks, thy lips, thy looks, speak all in order,

Thou think'st, and right thou think'st, that these
                    do move me,
That all these severally thy suit do further:
  But shall I tell thee what most thy suit advances?
  Thy fair smooth words? no, no, thy fair
                smooth haunches.

## Sonnet 2

When forty winters shall besiege thy brow
And dig deep trenches in thy beauty's field,
Thy youth's proud livery, so gazed on now,
Will be a tottered weed, of small worth held.
Then being asked where all thy beauty lies –
Where all the treasure of thy lusty days –
To say within thine own deep-sunken eyes
Were an all-eating shame and thriftless praise.
How much more praise deserved thy beauty's use,
If thou couldst answer 'This fair child of mine
Shall sum my count and make my old excuse –
Proving his beauty by succession thine.
    This were to be new made when thou art old,
    And see thy blood warm when thou feel'st it cold.

## *Sonnet 18*

Shall I compare thee to a summer's day?
Thou art more lovely and more temperate:
Rough winds do shake the darling buds of May,
And summer's lease hath all too short a date;
Sometime too hot the eye of heaven shines,
And often is his gold complexion dimm'd;
And every fair from fair sometime declines,
By chance or nature's changing course untrimm'd;
But thy eternal summer shall not fade,
Nor lose possession of that fair thou ow'st;
Nor shall death brag thou wander'st in his shade,
When in eternal lines to time thou grow'st:
   So long as men can breathe or eyes can see,
   So long lives this, and this gives life to thee.

WILLIAM SHAKESPEARE

## Sonnet 29

When, in disgrace with fortune and men's eyes,
I all alone beweep my outcast state,
And trouble deaf heaven with my bootless cries,
And look upon myself and curse my fate,
Wishing me like to one more rich in hope,
Featured like him, like him with friends possessed,
Desiring this man's art and that man's scope,
With what I most enjoy contented least;
Yet in these thoughts myself almost despising,
Haply I think on thee, and then my state,
(Like to the lark at break of day arising
From sullen earth) sings hymns at heaven's gate;
    For thy sweet love remembered such wealth brings
    That then I scorn to change my state with kings.

*Love Poetry*

WILLIAM SHAKESPEARE

## *Sonnet 55*

Not marble nor the gilded monuments
Of princes shall outlive this powerful rhyme;
But you shall shine more bright in these contents
Than unswept stone besmeared with sluttish time.
When wasteful war shall statues overturn,
And broils root out the work of masonry,
Nor Mars his sword nor war's quick fire shall burn
The living record of your memory.
'Gainst death and all-oblivious enmity
Shall you pace forth; your praise shall still find room
Even in the eyes of all posterity
That wear this world out to the ending doom.
   So, till the Judgement that yourself arise,
     You live in this, and dwell in lovers' eyes.

**WILLIAM SHAKESPEARE**

## *Sonnet 87*

Farewell! thou art too dear for my possessing,
And like enough thou knowst thy estimate.
The Charter of thy worth gives thee releasing;
My bonds in thee are all determinate.
For how do I hold thee but by thy granting,
And for that riches where is my deserving?
The cause of this fair gift in me is wanting,
And so my patent back again is swerving.
Thy self thou gav'st, thy own worth then not knowing,
Or me, to whom thou gav'st is, else mistaking,
So thy great gift, upon misprision growing,
Comes home again, on better judgement making.
   Thus have I had thee as a dream doth flatter:
   In sleep a king, but waking no such matter.

WILLIAM SHAKESPEARE

## Sonnet 98

From you have I been absent in the spring,
When proud-pied April, dressed in all his trim,
Hath put a spirit of youth in everything,
That heavy Saturn laughed and leaped with him.
Yet nor the lays of birds, nor the sweet smell
Of different flowers in odour and in hue,
Could make me any summer's story tell,
Or from their proud lap pluck them where they grew:
Nor did I wonder at the lily's white,
Nor praise the deep vermilion in the rose;
They were but sweet, but figures of delight
Drawn after you, – you pattern of all those.
 Yet seem'd it winter still, and, you away,
 As with your shadow I with these did play.

## *Sonnet 106*

When in the chronicle of wasted time
I see descriptions of the fairest wights,
And beauty making beautiful old rhyme
In praise of ladies dead and lovely knights,
Then, in the blazon of sweet beauty's best,
Of hand, of foot, of lip, of eye, of brow,
I see their antique pen would have expressed
Even such a beauty as you master now.
So all their praises are but prophecies
Of this our time, all you prefiguring;
And, for they looked but with divining eyes,
They had not skill enough your worth to sing:
   For we, which now behold these present days,
   Have eyes to wonder, but lack tongues to praise.

## *Sonnet 109*

O! never say that I was false of heart,
Though absence seemed my flame to qualify.
As easy might I from myself depart
As from my soul, which in thy breast doth lie:
That is my home of love; if I have ranged,
Like him that travels, I return again,
Just to the time, not with the time exchanged,
So that myself bring water for my stain.
Never believe, though in my nature reigned
All frailties that besiege all kinds of blood,
That it could so preposterously be stained,
To leave for nothing all thy sum of good;
    For nothing this wide universe I call,
    Save thou, my rose; in it thou art my all.

## *Sonnet 116*

Let me not to the marriage of true minds
Admit impediments. Love is not love
Which alters when it alteration finds,
Or bends with the remover to remove.
O no! it is an ever-fixed mark
That looks on tempests and is never shaken;
It is the star to every wand'ring bark,
Whose worth's unknown, although his height be taken.
Love's not Time's fool, though rosy lips and cheeks
Within his bending sickle's compass come;
Love alters not with his brief hours and weeks,
But bears it out even to the edge of doom.
    If this be error and upon me proved,
    I never writ, nor no man ever loved.

WILLIAM SHAKESPEARE

## *Sonnet 126*

O thou, my lovely boy, who in thy power
Dost hold time's fickle glass his sickle hour,
Who hast by waning grown, and therein show'st
Thy lovers withering, as thy sweet self grow'st –
In nature, sovereign mistress over wrack,
As thou goest onwards still will pluck thee back,
She keeps thee to this purpose, that her skill
May time disgrace, and wretched minute kill.
Yet fear her, O thou minion of her pleasure;
She may detain but not still keep her treasure.
   Her audit, though delayed, answered must be,
   And her quietus is to render thee.

## *Sonnet 129*

Th'expense of spirit in a waste of shame
Is lust in action; and till action, lust
Is perjured, murd'rous, bloody, full of blame,
Savage, extreme, rude, cruel, not to trust,
Enjoyed no sooner but despisèd straight,
Past reason hunted; and, no sooner had
Past reason hated as a swallowed bait
On purpose laid to make the taker mad;
Mad in pursuit and in possession so,
Had, having, and in quest to have, extreme;
A bliss in proof and proved, a very woe;
Before, a joy proposed; behind, a dream.
    All this the world well knows; yet none knows well
    To shun the heaven that leads men to this hell.

WILLIAM SHAKESPEARE

## Sonnet 130

My mistress' eyes are nothing like the sun;
Coral is far more red than her lips' red;
If snow be white, why then her breasts are dun;
If hairs be wires, black wires grow on her head.
I have seen roses damasked, red and white,
But no such roses see I in her cheeks;
And in some perfumes is there more delight
Than in the breath that from my mistress reeks.
I love to hear her speak, yet well I know
That music hath a far more pleasing sound;
I grant I never saw a goddess go;
My mistress, when she walks, treads on the ground:
    And yet, by heaven, I think my love as rare
    As any she belied with false compare.

## Sonnet 133

Beshrew that heart that makes my heart to groan
For that deep wound it gives my friend and me:
Is't not enough to torture me alone,
But slave to slavery my sweet'st friend must be?
Me from myself thy cruel eye hath taken,
And my next self thou harder hast engrossed;
Of him, myself, and thee I am forsaken,
A torment thrice threefold thus to be crossed.
Prison my heart in thy steel bosom's ward,
But then my friend's heart let my poor heart bail;
Whoe'er keeps me, let my heart be his guard:
Thou canst not then use rigour in my jail.
   And yet thou wilt; for I, being pent in thee,
   Perforce am thine, and all that is in me.

WILLIAM SHAKESPEARE

## Sonnet 137

Thou blind fool, Love, what dost thou to mine eyes,
That they behold, and see not what they see?
They know what beauty is, see where it lies,
Yet what the best is take the worst to be.
If eyes corrupt by over-partial looks
Be anchor'd in the bay where all men ride,
Why of eyes' falsehood hast thou forged hooks,
Whereto the judgment of my heart is tied?
Why should my heart think that a several plot
Which my heart knows the wide world's common place?
Or mine eyes seeing this, say this is not,
To put fair truth upon so foul a face?
   In things right true my heart and eyes have erred,
   And to this false plague are they now transferr'd.

# WILLIAM SHAKESPEARE

## *Sonnet 142*

Love is my sin, and thy dear virtue hate,
Hate of my sin, grounded on sinful loving.
O, but with mine compare thou thine own state,
And thou shalt find it merits not reproving;
Or if it do, not from those lips of thine,
That have profaned their scarlet ornaments
And sealed false bonds of love as oft as mine,
Robbed others' beds' revenues of their rents.
Be it lawful I love thee as thou lov'st those
Whom thine eyes woo as mine importune thee:
Root pity in thy heart, that, when it grows,
Thy pity may deserve to pitied be.
    If thou dost seek to have what thou dost hide,
    By self-example mayst thou be denied.

*Love Poetry*

## *Sonnet 147*

My love is a fever, longing still
For that which longer nurseth the disease,
Feeding on that which doth preserve the ill,
Th'uncertain sickly appetite to please.
My reason, the physician to my love,
Angry that his prescriptions are not kept,
Hath left me, and I desperate now approve
Desire is death, which physic did except.
Past cure I am, now reason is past care,
And frantic-mad with evermore unrest;
My thoughts and my discourse as madmen's are,
At random from the truth vainly expressed:
    For I have sworn thee fair, and thought thee bright,
    Who art as black as hell, as dark as night.

## *I Saw My Lady Weep*

I saw my Lady weep,
And Sorrow proud to be advanced so
In those fair eyes, where all perfections keep;
   Her face was full of woe,
But such a woe (believe me) as wins more hearts
Than mirth can do, with her enticing parts.

Sorrow was there made fair,
And Passion, wise; Tears, a delightful thing;
Silence, beyond all speech, a wisdom rare;
   She made her sighs to sing,
And all things with so sweet a sadness move;
As made my heart both grieve and love.

O Fairer than aught else
The world can shew, leave off, in time, to grieve,
Enough, enough! Your joyful look excels;
   Tears kill the heart, believe,
O strive not to be excellent in woe,
Which only breeds your beauty's overthrow.

## SIR WALTER RALEGH

### *The Nymph's Reply to the Shepherd*

If all the world and love were young,
And truth in every Shepherd's tongue,
These pretty pleasures might me move,
To live with thee, and be thy love.

Time drives the flocks from field to fold,
When Rivers rage and Rocks grow cold,
And Philomel becometh dumb,
The rest complains of cares to come.

The flowers do fade, and wanton fields,
To wayward winter reckoning yields,
A honey tongue, a heart of gall,
Is fancy's spring, but sorrow's fall.

Thy gowns, thy shoes, thy beds of Roses,
Thy cap, thy kirtle, and thy posies
Soon break, soon wither, soon forgotten:
In folly ripe, in reason rotten.

Thy belt of straw and Ivy buds,
The Coral clasps and amber studs,
All these in me no means can move
To come to thee and be thy love.

But could youth last, and love still breed,
Had joys no date, nor age no need,
Then these delights my mind might move
To live with thee, and be thy love.

## *A Farewell to False Love*

Farewell, false love, the oracle of lies,
A mortal foe and enemy to rest,
An envious boy, from whom all cares arise,
A bastard vile, a beast with rage possessed,
A way of error, a temple full of treason,
In all effects contrary unto reason.

A poisoned serpent covered all with flowers,
Mother of sighs, and murderer of repose,
A sea of sorrows whence are drawn such showers
As moisture lend to every grief that grows;
A school of guile, a net of deep deceit,
A gilded hook that holds a poisoned bait.

A fortress foiled, which reason did defend,
A siren song, a fever of the mind,
A maze wherein affection finds no end,
A raging cloud that runs before the wind,
A substance like the shadow of the sun,
A goal of grief for which the wisest run.

A quenchless fire, a nurse of trembling fear,
A path that leads to peril and mishap,
A true retreat of sorrow and despair,
An idle boy that sleeps in pleasure's lap,
A deep mistrust of that which certain seems,
A hope of that which reason doubtful deems.

Sith then thy trains my younger years betrayed,
And for my faith ingratitude I find;

And sith repentance hath my wrongs bewrayed,
Whose course was ever contrary to kind:
False love, desire, and beauty frail, adieu!
Dead is the root whence all these fancies grew.

SIR WALTER RALEGH

### A Vision upon the Fairy Queen

Methought I saw the grave where Laura lay,
Within that temple where the vestal flame
Was wont to burn; and, passing by that way,
To see that buried dust of living fame,
Whose tomb fair Love, and fairer Virtue kept:
All suddenly I saw the Fairy Queen;
At whose approach the soul of Petrarch wept,
And, from thenceforth, those Graces were not seen:
For they this queen attended; in whose stead
Oblivion laid him down on Laura's hearse:
Hereat the hardest stones were seen to bleed,
And groans of buried ghosts the heavens did pierce:
Where Homer's spright did tremble all for grief,
And cursed the access of that celestial thief!

**SIR WALTER RALEGH**

## *Prais'd be Diana's Fair and Harmless Light*

Prais'd be Diana's fair and harmless light;
Prais'd be the dews wherewith she moists the ground;
Prais'd be her beams, the glory of the night;
Prais'd be her power by which all powers abound.

Prais'd be her nymphs with whom she decks the
woods,
Prais'd be her knights in whom true honour lives;
Prais'd be that force by which she moves the floods;
Let that Diana shine which all these gives.

In heaven queen she is among the spheres;
In aye she mistress-like makes all things pure;
Eternity in her oft change she bears;
She beauty is; by her the fair endure.

Time wears her not: she doth his chariot guide;
Mortality below her orb is plac'd;
By her the virtue of the stars down slide;
In her is virtue's perfect image cast.

  A knowledge pure it is her worth to know:
  With Circes let them dwell that think not so.

## SIR WALTER RALEGH

### *Walsingham*

'As you came from the holy land
    Of Walsingham,
Met you not with my true love
    By the way as you came?'

'How shall I know your true love,
    That have met many one,
As I went to the holy land,
    That have come, that have gone?'

'She is neither white, nor brown,
    But as the heavens fair;
There is none hath a form so divine
    In the earth, or the air.'

'Such a one did I meet, good Sir,
    Such an angelic face,
Who like a queen, like a nymph, did appear
    By her gait, by her grace.'

'She hath left me here all alone,
    All alone, as unknown,
Who sometimes did me lead with herself,
    And me loved as her own.'

'What's the cause that she leaves you alone,
    And a new way doth take,
Who loved you once as her own,
    And her joy did you make?'

I have loved her all my youth;
  But now old, as you see,
Love likes not the falling fruit
  From the withered tree.

Know that Love is a careless child,
  And forgets promise past;
He is blind, he is deaf when he list,
  And in faith never fast.

His desire is a dureless content,
  And a trustless joy:
He is won with a world of despair,
  And is lost with a toy.

Of womenkind such indeed is the love,
  Or the word love abused,
Under which many childish desires
  And conceits are excused.

But true love is a durable fire,
  In the mind ever burning,
Never sick, never old, never dead,
  From itself never turning.

*Love Poetry*

## THOMAS CAMPION

### *Cherry-Ripe*

There is a garden in her face
   Where roses and white lilies blow;
A heavenly paradise is that place,
   Wherein all pleasant fruits do flow:
     There cherries grow which none may buy
     Till 'Cherry-ripe' themselves do cry.

Those cherries fairly do enclose
   Of orient pearls a double row,
Which when her lovely laughter shows,
   They look like rose-buds filled with snow;
     Yet them no peer nor prince can buy
     Till 'Cherry-ripe' themselves do cry.

Her eyes like angels watch them still;
   Her brows like bended bows do stand,
Threatening with piercing frowns to kill
   All that attempt with eye or hand
     Those sacred cherries to come nigh,
     Till 'Cherry-ripe' themselves do cry.

## THOMAS CAMPION

### *Vobiscum Est Iope*

When thou must home to shades of underground,
And there arrived, a new admirèd guest,
The beauteous spirits do engirt thee round,
White Iope, blithe Helen, and the rest,
To hear the stories of thy finished love
From that smooth tongue whose music hell can move;

Then wilt thou speak of banqueting delights,
Of masques and revels which sweet youth did make,
Of tourneys and great challenges of knights,
And all these triumphs for thy beauty's sake:
When thou hast told these honours done to thee,
Then tell, O tell, how thou didst murder me!

THOMAS CAMPION

## Kind are Her Answers

Kind are her answers,
But her performance keeps no day;
Breaks time, as dancers
From their own music when they stray:
All her free favours
And smooth words wing my hopes in vain.
O did ever voice so sweet but only feign?
Can true love yield such delay,
Converting joy to pain?

Lost is our freedom,
When we submit to women so:
Why do we need 'em,
When in their best they work our woe?
There is no wisdom
Can alter ends, by Fate prefixed.
O why is the good of man with evil mixed?
Never were days yet called two,
But one night went betwixt.

## Love's Emblems

Now the lusty spring is seen;
  Golden yellow, gaudy blue,
  Daintily invite the view:
Everywhere on every green
Roses blushing as they blow,
  And enticing men to pull,
Lilies whiter than the snow,
  Woodbines of sweet honey full:
  All love's emblems, and all cry,
  'Ladies, if not pluck'd, we die.'

Yet the lusty spring hath stayed;
  Blushing red and purest white
  Daintily to love invite
Every woman, every maid:
Cherries kissing as they grow,
  And inviting men to taste,
Apples even ripe below,
  Winding gently to the waist:
  All love's emblems, and all cry,
  'Ladies, if not pluck'd, we die.'

## Song

Sweetest love, I do not go,
    For weariness of thee,
Nor in hope the world can show
    A fitter love for me;
        But since that I
Must die at last, 'tis best
To use myself in jest
        Thus by feign'd deaths to die.

Yesternight the sun went hence,
    And yet is here today;
He hath no desire nor sense,
    Nor half so short a way:
        Then fear not me,
But believe that I shall make
Speedier journeys, since I take
        More wings and spurs than he.

O how feeble is man's power,
    That if good fortune fall,
Cannot add another hour,
    Nor a lost hour recall!
        But come bad chance,
And we join to it our strength,
And we teach it art and length,
        Itself o'er us to advance.

When thou sigh'st, thou sigh'st not wind,
    But sigh'st my soul away;
When thou weep'st, unkindly kind,

My life's blood doth decay.
　　　　It cannot be
That thou lov'st me, as thou say'st,
If in thine my life thou waste,
　　　　That art the best of me.

Let not thy divining heart
　　　　Forethink me any ill;
Destiny may take thy part,
　　　　And may thy fears fulfil;
　　　　　　But think that we
Are but turned aside to sleep;
They who one another keep
　　　　Alive, ne'er parted be.

## The Good-Morrow

I wonder, by my troth, what thou and I
Did, till we loved? Were we not weaned till then?
But sucked on country pleasures, childishly?
Or snorted we in the Seven Sleepers' den?
'Twas so; but this, all pleasures fancies be.
If ever any beauty I did see,
Which I desired, and got, 'twas but a dream of thee.

And now good-morrow to our waking souls,
Which watch not one another out of fear;
For love, all love of other sights controls,
And makes one little room an everywhere.
Let sea-discoverers to new worlds have gone,
Let maps to other, worlds on worlds have shown,
Let us possess one world, each hath one, and is one.

My face in thine eye, thine in mine appears,
And true plain hearts do in the faces rest;
Where can we find two better hemispheres,
Without sharp north, without declining west?
Whatever dies, was not mixed equally;
If our two loves be one, or, thou and I
Love so alike, that none do slacken, none can die.

JOHN DONNE

## *The Canonisation*

For God's sake hold your tongue, and let me love,
    Or chide my palsy, or my gout,
My five gray hairs, or ruined fortune flout,
    With wealth your state, your mind
                    with arts improve,
        Take you a course, get you a place,
        Observe his honour, or his grace,
Or the king's real, or his stamped face
    Contemplate; what you will, approve,
    So you will let me love.

Alas, alas, who's injured by my love?
    What merchant's ships have my sighs drowned?
Who says my tears have overflowed his ground?
    When did my colds a forward spring remove?
        When did the heats which my veins fill
        Add one more to the plaguy bill?
Soldiers find wars, and lawyers find out still
    Litigious men, which quarrels move,
    Though she and I do love.

Call us what you will, we are made such by love;
    Call her one, me another fly,
We're tapers too, and at our own cost die,
    And we in us find the eagle and the dove.
        The phoenix riddle hath more wit
        By us; we two being one, are it.
So to one neutral thing both sexes fit.
    We die and rise the same, and prove
    Mysterious by this love.

We can die by it, if not live by love,
    And if unfit for tombs and hearse
Our legend be, it will be fit for verse;
    And if no piece of chronicle we prove,
        We'll build in sonnets pretty rooms;
        As well a well-wrought urn becomes
The greatest ashes, as half-acre tombs,
    And by these hymns, all shall approve
    Us canonised for love.

And thus invoke us: 'You, whom reverend love
    Made one another's hermitage;
You, to whom love was peace, that now is rage;
    Who did the whole world's soul contract, and drove
        Into the glasses of your eyes
        (So made such mirrors, and such spies,
That they did all to you epitomise)
    Countries, towns, courts: beg from above
    A pattern of your love!'

## JOHN DONNE

### *Woman's Constancy*

Now thou has loved me one whole day,
Tomorrow when you leav'st, what wilt thou say?
Wilt thou then antedate some new-made vow?
     Or say that now
We are not just those persons which we were?
Or, that oaths made in reverential fear
Of Love, and his wrath, any may forswear?
Or, as true deaths true marriages untie,
So lovers' contracts, images of those,
Bind but till sleep, death's image, them unloose?
     Or, your own end to justify,
For having purposed change and falsehood, you
Can have no way but falsehood to be true?
Vain lunatic, against these 'scapes I could
     Dispute and conquer, if I would,
      Which I abstain to do,
For by tomorrow, I may think so too.

JOHN DONNE

## The Expiration

So, so, break off this last lamenting kiss,
   Which sucks two souls, and vapours Both away,
Turn thou ghost that way, and let me turn this,
   And let our selves benight our happiest day,
We ask'd none leave to love; nor will we owe
   Any, so cheap a death, as saying, Go;

Go; and if that word have not quite kill'd thee,
   Ease me with death, by bidding me go too.
Oh, if it have, let my word work on me,
   And a just office on a murderer do.
Except it be too late, to kill me so,
   Being double dead, going, and bidding, go.

## JOHN DONNE

### (Elegy 19)

## To His Mistress Going to Bed

Come, Madam, come, all rest my powers defy,
Until I labour, I in labour lie.
The foe oft-times having the foe in sight,
Is tir'd with standing though he never fight.
Off with that girdle, like heaven's Zone glistering,
But a far fairer world encompassing.
Unpin that spangled breastplate which you wear,
That th'eyes of busy fools may be stopped there.
Unlace yourself, for that harmonious chime,
Tells me from you, that now it is bed time.
Off with that happy busk, which I envy,
That still can be, and still can stand so nigh.
Your gown going off, such beauteous state reveals,
As when from flowery meads th'hill's shadow steals.
Off with that wiry Coronet and shew
The hairy Diadem which on you doth grow:
Now off with those shoes, and then safely tread
In this love's hallow'd temple, this soft bed.
In such white robes, heaven's Angels used to be
Received by men; Thou Angel bringst with thee
A heaven like Mahomet's Paradise; and though
Ill spirits walk in white, we easily know,
By this these Angels from an evil sprite,
Those set our hairs, but these our flesh upright.
     Licence my roving hands, and let them go,
Before, behind, between, above, below.
O my America! my new-found-land,
My kingdom, safeliest when with one man mann'd,

         *Love Poetry*

My Mine of precious stones, My Empirie,
How blest am I in this discovering thee!
To enter in these bonds, is to be free;
Then where my hand is set, my seal shall be.

Full nakedness! All joys are due to thee,
As souls unbodied, bodies uncloth'd must be,
To taste whole joys. Gems which you women use
Are like Atlanta's balls, cast in men's views,
That when a fool's eye lighteth on a Gem,
His earthly soul may covet theirs, not them.
Like pictures, or like books' gay coverings made
For lay-men, are all women thus array'd;
Themselves are mystic books, which only we
(Whom their imputed grace will dignify)
Must see reveal'd. Then since that I may know;
As liberally, as to a Midwife, shew
Thy self: cast all, yea, this white linen hence,
There is no penance due to innocence.

To teach thee, I am naked first; why then
What needst thou have more covering than a man.

*Air and Angels*

Twice or thrice had I lov'd thee,
Before I knew thy face or name;
So in a voice, so in a shapeless flame
Angels affect us oft, and worshipp'd be;
   Still when, to where thou wert, I came,
Some lovely glorious nothing I did see.
   But since my soul, whose child love is,
Takes limbs of flesh, and else could nothing do,
   More subtle than the parent is
Love must not be, but take a body too;
   And therefore what thou wert, and who,
     I bid Love ask, and now
That it assume thy body, I allow,
And fix itself in thy lip, eye, and brow.

Whilst thus to ballast love I thought,
And so more steadily to have gone,
With wares which would sink admiration,
I saw I had love's pinnace overfraught;
   Ev'ry thy hair for love to work upon
Is much too much, some fitter must be sought;
   For, nor in nothing, nor in things
Extreme, and scatt'ring bright, can love inhere;
   Then, as an angel, face, and wings
Of air, not pure as it, yet pure, doth wear,
   So thy love may be my love's sphere;
     Just such disparity
As is 'twixt air and angels' purity,
'Twixt women's love, and men's, will ever be.

JOHN DONNE

*The Ecstasy*

Where, like a pillow on a bed
    A pregnant bank swell'd up to rest
The violet's reclining head,
    Sat we two, one another's best.

Our hands were firmly cemented
    With a fast balm, which thence did spring;
Our eye-beams twisted, and did thread
    Our eyes upon one double string;

So to entergraft our hands, as yet
    Was all the means to make us one,
And pictures in our eyes to get
    Was all our propagation.

As 'twixt two equal armies, Fate
    Suspends uncertain victory,
Our souls (which to advance their state
    Were gone out) hung 'twixt her and me.

And whilst our souls negotiate there,
    We like sepulchral statues lay;
All day, the same our postures were,
    And we said nothing, all the day.

If any, so by love refined
    That he soul's language understood,
And by good love were grown all mind,
    Within convenient distance stood,

He (though he knew not which soul spake,
    Because both meant, both spake the same)
Might thence a new concoction take
    And part far purer than he came.

This ecstasy doth unperplex,
    We said, and tell us what we love;
We see by this it was not sex,
    We see, we saw not what did move;

But as all several souls contain
    Mixture of things, they know not what,
Love these mixed souls doth mix again
    And makes both one, each this and that.

A single violet transplant,
    The strength, the colour, and the size,
(All which before was poor and scant)
    Redoubles still, and multiplies.
When love with one another so
    Interinanimates two souls,
That abler soul, which thence doth flow,
    Defects of loneliness controls.

We then, who are this new soul, know
    Of what we are composed and made,
For the atomies of which we grow
    Are souls, whom no change can invade.

But O alas! so long, so far,
    Our bodies why do we forbear?
They are ours, though they are not we; we are
    The intelligences, they the sphere.

We owe them thanks, because they thus
    Did us, to us, at first convey,
Yielded their forces, sense, force to us,
    Nor are dross to us, but allay.

On man heaven's influence works not so,
    But that it first imprints the air;
So soul into the soul may flow,
    Though it to body first repair.

As our blood labours to beget
    Spirits, as like souls as it can,
Because such fingers need to knit
    That subtle knot which makes us man;

So must pure lovers' souls descend
    To affections, and to faculties,
Which sense may reach and apprehend,
    Else a great prince in prison lies.

To our bodies turn we then, that so
    Weak men on love revealed may look;
Love's mysteries in souls do grow,
    But yet the body is his book.

And if some lover, such as we,
    Have heard this dialogue of one,
Let him still mark us, he shall see
    Small change, when we're to bodies gone.

## The Bait

Come live with me, and be my love,
And we will some new pleasures prove
Of golden sands, and crystal brooks,
With silken lines, and silver hooks.

There will the river whispering run
Warm'd by thy eyes, more than the sun;
And there th'enamour'd fish will stay,
Begging themselves they may betray.

When thou wilt swim in that live bath,
Each fish, which every channel hath,
Will amorously to thee swim,
Gladder to catch thee, than thou him.

If thou, to be so seen, be'st loth,
By sun or moon, thou dark'nest both,
And if myself have leave to see,
I need not their light having thee.

Let others freeze with angling reeds,
And cut their legs with shells and weeds,
Or treacherously poor fish beset,
With strangling snare, or windowy net.

Let coarse bold hands from slimy nest
The bedded fish in banks out-wrest;
Or curious traitors, sleeve-silk flies,
Bewitch poor fishes' wand'ring eyes.

For thee, thou need'st no such deceit,
For thou thyself art thine own bait:
That fish, that is not catch'd thereby,
Alas, is wiser far than I.


JOHN DONNE

*The Indifferent*

I can love both fair and brown,
Her whom abundance melts, and her whom
                      want betrays,
Her who loves loneness best, and her who masks
                      and plays,
Her whom the country formed, and whom
                      the town,
Her who believes, and her who tries,
Her who still weeps with spongy eyes,
And her who is dry cork, and never cries;
I can love her, and her, and you, and you,
I can love any, so she be not true.


Will no other vice content you?
Will it not serve your turn to do as did your mothers?
Or have you all old vices spent, and now would
                      find out others?
Or doth a fear that men are true torment you?
O we are not, be not you so;
Let me, and do you, twenty know.
Rob me, but bind me not, and let me go.
Must I, who came to travail thorough you,
Grow your fixed subject, because you are true?

Venus heard me sigh this song,
And by love's sweetest part, variety, she swore,
She heard not this till now; and that it should be
                                        so no more.
    She went, examined, and returned ere long,
        And said, Alas! some two or three
        Poor heretics in love there be,
    Which think to 'stablish dangerous constancy.
But I have told them, Since you will be true,
You shall be true to them who are false to you.

*Love Poetry*

MICHAEL DRAYTON

## Sonnet 59

As Love and I, late harbour'd in one inn,
With proverbs thus each other entertain:
In love there is no lack, thus I begin,
Fair words make fools, replieth he again;
Who spares to speak, doth spare to speed (quoth I),
As well (saith he) too forward, as too slow;
Fortune assists the boldest, I reply,
A hasty man (quoth he) ne'er wanted woe;
Labour is light, where love (quoth I) doth pay,
(Saith he) light burthen's heavy, if far born;
(Quoth I) the main lost, cast the bye away;
You have spun a fair thread, he replies in scorn.
    And having thus awhile each other thwarted,
      Fools as we met, so fools again we parted.

## MICHAEL DRAYTON

### Sonnet 61

Since there's no help, come let us kiss and part,
Nay, I have done, you get no more of me,
And I am glad, yea, glad with all my heart,
That thus so cleanly I myself can free.
Shake hands for ever, cancel all our vows,
And when we meet at any time again
Be it not seen in either of our brows
That we one jot of former love retain.
Now at the last gasp of Love's latest breath,
When, his pulse failing, Passion speechless lies,
When Faith is kneeling by his bed of death,
And Innocence is closing up his eyes,
  Now, if thou would'st, when all have given him over,
  From death to life thou might'st him yet recover.

### GEORGE HERBERT

## Love

Love bade me welcome: yet my soul drew back,
    Guilty of dust and sin.
But quick-eyed Love, observing me grow slack
    From my first entrance in,
Drew nearer to me, sweetly questioning
    If I lacked anything.

'A guest,' I answered, 'worthy to be here':
    Love said, 'You shall be he.'
'I, the unkind, ungrateful? Ah, my dear,
    I cannot look on thee.'
Love took my hand, and smiling did reply,
    'Who made the eyes but I?'

'Truth, Lord; but I have marred them; let my shame
    Go where it doth deserve.'
'And know you not,' says Love, 'who bore the blame?'
    'My dear, then I will serve.'
'You must sit down,' says Love, 'and taste my meat.'
    So I did sit and eat.

THOMAS RANDOLPH

## The Milkmaid's Epithalamium

Joy to the bridegroom and the bride
That lie by one another's side!
O fie upon the virgin beds,
No loss is gain but maidenheads.
Love quickly send the time may be
When I shall deal my rosemary!

I long to simper at a feast,
To dance, and kiss, and do the rest.
When I shall wed, and bedded be
O then the qualm comes over me,
And tells the sweetness of a theme
That I ne'er knew but in a dream.

You ladies have the blessed nights,
I pine in hope of such delights.
And silly damsel only can
Milk the cows' teats and think on man:
And sigh and wish to taste and prove
The wholesome sillabub of love.

Make haste, at once twin-brothers bear;
And leave new matter for a star.
Women and ships are never shown
So fair as when their sails be blown.
Then when the midwife hears your moan,
I'll sigh for grief that I have none.

And you, dear knight, whose every kiss
Reaps the full crop of Cupid's bliss,

Now you have found, confess and tell
That single sheets do make up hell.
And then so charitable be
To get a man to pity me.

SIR HENRY WOTTON

*Upon the Death of Sir Albert Morton's Wife*

He first deceased; she for a little tried
To live without him, liked it not, and died.

## BEN JONSON

### *Song to Celia*

Drink to me only with thine eyes,
    And I will pledge with mine;
Or leave a kiss but in the cup,
    And I'll not look for wine.
The thirst that from the soul doth rise
    Doth ask a drink divine;
But might I of Jove's nectar sup,
    I would not change for thine.

I sent thee late a rosy wreath,
    Not so much honouring thee
As giving it a hope, that there
    It could not withered be.
But thou thereon didst only breathe,
    And sent'st it back to me;
Since when it grows, and smells, I swear,
    Not of itself, but thee.

## THOMAS CAREW

### FROM *A Rapture*

I will enjoy thee now, my Celia, come,
And fly with me to Love's Elysium.
The giant, Honour, that keeps cowards out,
Is but a masquer, and the servile rout
Of baser subjects only bend in vain
To the vast idol; whilst the nobler train
Of valiant lovers daily sail between
The huge Colossus' legs, and pass unseen
Unto the blissful shore. Be bold and wise,
And we shall enter: the grim Swiss denies
Only to tame fools a passage, that not know
He is but form and only frights in show
The duller eyes that look from far; draw near
And thou shalt scorn what we were wont to fear.
We shall see how the stalking pageant goes
With borrow'd legs, a heavy load to those
That made and bear him; not, as we once thought,
The seed of gods, but a weak model wrought
By greedy men, that seek to enclose the common,
And within private arms empale free woman.
      Come, then, and mounted on the wings of Love
We'll cut the flitting air and soar above
The monster's head, and in the noblest seats
Of those blest shades quench and renew our heats.
There shall the queens of love and innocence,
Beauty and Nature, banish all offence
From our close ivy-twines; there I'll behold
Thy bared snow and thy unbraided gold;
There my enfranchised hand on every side
Shall o'er thy naked polish'd ivory slide.

No curtain there, though of transparent lawn,
Shall be before thy virgin-treasure drawn;
But the rich mine, to the enquiring eye
Exposed, shall ready still for mintage lie,
And we will coin young Cupids. There a bed
Of roses and fresh myrtles shall be spread,
Under the cooler shade of cypress groves;
Our pillows of the down of Venus' doves,
Whereon our panting limbs we'll gently lay,
In the faint respites of our active play:
That so our slumbers may in dreams have leisure
To tell the nimble fancy our past pleasure,
And so our souls, that cannot be embraced,
Shall the embraces of our bodies taste.
Meanwhile the bubbling stream shall court the shore,
Th'enamour'd chirping wood-choir shall adore
In varied tunes the deity of love;
The gentle blasts of western winds shall move
The trembling leaves, and through their close
                                    boughs breathe
Still music, whilst we rest ourselves beneath
Their dancing shade; till a soft murmur, sent
From souls entranced in amorous languishment,
Rouse us, and shoot into our veins fresh fire,
Till we in their sweet ecstasy expire.

THOMAS CAREW

## A Song

Ask me no more where Jove bestows,
When June is past, the fading rose;
For in your beauty's orient deep
These flowers, as in their causes, sleep.

Ask me no more whither do stray
The golden atoms of the day;
For in pure love heaven did prepare
Those powders to enrich your hair.

Ask me no more whither doth haste
The nightingale, when May is past;
For in your sweet dividing throat
She winters and keeps warm her note.

Ask me no more where those stars 'light
That downwards fall in dead of night;
For in your eyes they sit, and there,
Fixed become as in their sphere.

Ask me no more if east or west
The phoenix builds her spicy nest;
For unto you at last she flies,
And in your fragrant bosom dies.

THOMAS CAREW

## On the Marriage of T. K. and C. C.

*(The Morning Stormy)*

Such should this day be, so the sun should hide
His bashful face, and let the conquering Bride
Without a rival shine, whilst he forbears
To mingle his unequal beams with hers;
Or if sometimes he glance his squinting eye
Between the parting clouds, 'tis but to spy,
Not emulate her glories, so comes dressed
In veils, but as a masquer to the feast.
Thus heaven should lower, such stormy gusts should blow
Not to denounce ungentle Fates, but show
The cheerful Bridegroom to the clouds and wind
Hath all his tears, and all his sighs assigned.
Let tempests struggle in the air, but rest
Eternal calms within thy peaceful breast,
Thrice happy Youth; but ever sacrifice
To that fair hand that dried thy blubbered eyes,
That crowned thy head with roses, and turned all
The plagues of love into a cordial,
When first it joined her virgin snow to thine,
Which when today the Priest shall recombine,
From the mysterious holy touch such charms
Will flow, as shall unlock her wreathèd arms,
And open a free passage to that fruit
Which thou hast toiled for with a long pursuit.
But ere thou feed, that thou may'st better taste
Thy present joys, think on thy torments past.
Think on the mercy freed thee, think upon
Her virtues, graces, beauties, one by one,

So shalt thou relish all, enjoy the whole
Delights of her fair body, and pure soul.
Then boldly to the fight of love proceed,
'Tis mercy not to pity though she bleed,
We'll strew no nuts, but change that ancient form,
For till tomorrow we'll prorogue this storm,
Which shall confound with its loud whistling noise
Her pleasing shrieks, and fan thy panting joys.


SIR JOHN SUCKLING

## Song

Why so pale and wan, fond lover?
    Prithee, why so pale?
Will, when looking well can't move her,
    Looking ill prevail?
    Prithee, why so pale?

Why so dull and mute, young sinner?
    Prithee, why so mute?
Will, when speaking well can't win her,
    Saying nothing do't?
    Prithee, why so mute?

Quit, quit for shame! This will not move;
    This cannot take her.
If of herself she will not love,
    Nothing can make her:
    The devil take her!

### SIR THOMAS WYATT

## *Alas! Madam, for Stealing of a Kiss*

Alas! madam, for stealing of a kiss
   Have I so much your mind there offended?
Have I then done so grievously amiss
   That by no means it may be amended?

Then revenge you, and the next way is this:
   Another kiss shall have my life ended,
For to my mouth the first my heart did suck;
   The next shall clean out of my breast it pluck.

### SIR THOMAS WYATT

## *Farewell Love and all Thy Laws Forever*

Farewell love and all thy laws forever;
Thy baited hooks shall tangle me no more.
Senec and Plato call me from thy lore
To perfect wealth, my wit for to endeavour.
In blind error when I did persever,
Thy sharp repulse, that pricketh aye so sore,
Hath taught me to set in trifles no store
And scape forth, since liberty is lever.
Therefore farewell; go trouble younger hearts
And in me claim no more authority.
With idle youth go use thy property
And thereon spend thy many brittle darts,
For hitherto though I have lost all my time,
Me lusteth no longer rotten boughs to climb.

           *Love Poetry*

SIR THOMAS WYATT

## *Forget not Yet the Tried Intent*

Forget not yet the tried intent
Of such a truth as I have meant;
My great travail so gladly spent,
    Forget not yet.

Forget not yet when first began
The weary life ye know, since whan
The suit, the service, none tell can;
    Forget not yet.

Forget not yet the great assays,
The cruel wrong, the scornful ways;
The painful patience in denays,
    Forget not yet.

Forget not yet, forget not this,
How long ago hath been and is
The mind that never meant amiss;
    Forget not yet.

Forget not then thine own approved,
The which so long hath thee so loved,
Whose steadfast faith yet never moved;
    Forget not this.

### SIR THOMAS WYATT

## *Remembrance*

They flee from me, that sometime did me seek
   With naked foot, stalking in my chamber.
I have seen them gentle, tame, and meek,
   That now are wild, and do not remember
   That sometime they put themselves in danger
      To take bread at my hand; and now they range
      Busily seeking with a continual change.

Thanked be fortune it hath been otherwise
   Twenty times better; but once, in special,
In thin array, after a pleasant guise,
   When her loose gown from her shoulders did fall,
   And she me caught in her arms long and small;
      Therewith all sweetly did me kiss,
      And softly said, 'Dear heart, how like you this?'

It was no dream: I lay broad waking:
   But all is turned, thorough my gentleness,
Into a strange fashion of forsaking;
   And I have leave to go of her goodness,
   And she also to use newfangleness.
      But since that I so kindly am served,
      I would fain know what she hath deserved.

SIR THOMAS WYATT

## *I Abide and Abide and Better Abide*

I abide and abide and better abide,
And after the old proverb, the happy day;
And ever my lady to me doth say,
'Let me alone and I will provide'.
I abide and abide and tarry the tide,
And with abiding speed well ye may!
Thus do I abide I wot alway,
Nother obtaining nor yet denied.
Ay me! this long abiding
Seemeth to me as who sayeth,
A prolonging of a dying death,
Or a refusing of a desired thing.
Much were it better for to be plain
Than to say 'abide' and yet not obtain.

WILLIAM DRUMMOND OF HAWTHORNDEN

## *I Know that All Beneath the Moon Decays*

I know that all beneath the moon decays,
And what by mortals in this world is brought,
In Time's great periods shall return to nought;
That fairest states have fatal nights and days;
I know how all the Muse's heavenly lays,
With toil of spright which are so dearly bought,
As idle sounds of few or none are sought,
And that nought lighter is than airy praise.
I know frail beauty like the purple flower,
To which one morn oft birth and death affords;
That love a jarring is of minds' accords,
Where sense and will invassal reason's power:
Know what I list, this all can not me move,
But that, O me! I both must write and love.

RICHARD LOVELACE

## The Scrutiny

Why should you swear I am forsworn,
    Since thine I vowed to be?
Lady, it is already morn,
    And 'twas last night I swore to thee
That fond impossibility.

Have I not loved thee much and long,
    A tedious twelve hours' space?
I must all other beauties wrong,
    And rob thee of a new embrace;
Could I still dote upon thy face.

Not, but all joy in thy brown hair,
    By others may be found;
But I must search the black and fair,
    Like skilful mineralists that sound
For treasure in unploughed-up ground.

Then, if when I have loved my round,
    Thou provest the pleasant she;
With spoils of meaner beauties crowned
    I laden will return to thee,
Ev'n sated with variety.

### RICHARD LOVELACE

## *To Lucasta, Going to the Wars*

Tell me not (Sweet) I am unkind,
  That from the nunnery
Of thy chaste breast and quiet mind
  To war and arms I fly.

True, a new mistress now I chase,
  The first foe in the field;
And with a stronger faith embrace
  A sword, a horse, a shield.

Yet this inconstancy is such
  As you too shall adore;
I could not love thee (Dear) so much,
  Loved I not Honour more.

## To Mrs M. A. Upon Absence

'Tis now since I began to die
   Four months, yet still I gasping live;
Wrapp'd up in sorrow do I lie,
   Hoping, yet doubting a reprieve.
Adam from Paradise expell'd
Just such a wretched being held.

'Tis not thy love I fear to lose,
   That will in spite of absence hold;
But 'tis the benefit and use
   Is lost, as in imprison'd gold:
Which though the sum be ne'er so great,
Enriches nothing but conceit.

What angry star then governs me
   That I must feel a double smart,
Prisoner to fate as well as thee;
   Kept from thy face, link'd to thy heart?
Because my love all love excels,
Must my grief have no parallels?

Sapless and dead as Winter here
   I now remain, and all I see
Copies of my wild state appear,
   But I am their epitome.
Love me no more, for I am grown
Too dead and dull for thee to own.

## SIR RICHARD FANSHAWE

### *Of Beauty*

Let us use it while we may
Snatch those joys that haste away!
Earth her winter coat may cast,
And renew her beauty past:
But, our winter come, in vain
We solicit spring again;
And when our furrows snow shall cover,
Love may return but never lover.

## A Lover's Resolution

Shall I, wasting in despair,
Die because a woman's fair?
Or make pale my cheeks with care
'Cause another's rosy are?
Be she fairer than the day,
Or the flowery meads in May,
　　If she be not so to me,
　　What care I how fair she be?

Shall my heart be grieved or pined
'Cause I see a woman kind?
Or a well disposed nature
Joined with a lovely feature?
Be she meeker, kinder, than
Turtle-dove or pelican,
　　If she be not so to me,
　　What care I how kind she be?

Shall a woman's virtues move
Me to perish for her love?
Or her well-deserving known
Make me quite forget my own?
Be she with that goodness blessed
Which may merit name of Best,
　　If she be not such to me,
　　What care I how good she be?

'Cause her fortune seems too high,
Shall I play the fool and die?
She that bears a noble mind,

Where they want of riches find,
Thinks what with them he would do
That without them dare to woo;
    And unless that mind I see,
    What care I though great she be?

Great, or good, or kind, or fair,
I will ne'er the more despair;
If she love me, this believe,
I will die ere she shall grieve;
If she slight me when I woo,
I can scorn and let her go;
    For if she be not for me,
    What care I for whom she be?

## Platonic Love

Indeed I must confess,
   When souls mix 'tis an happiness,
But not complete till bodies too do join,
And both our wholes into one whole combine;
But half of heaven the souls in glory taste
   Till by love in heaven at last
   Their bodies too are placed.

   In thy immortal part
   Man, as well as I, thou art.
But something 'tis that differs thee and me,
And we must one even in that difference be.
I thee both as a man and woman prise,
   For a perfect love implies
   Love in all capacities.

   Can that for true love pass
   When a fair woman courts her glass?
Something unlike must in love's likeness be:
His wonder is one and variety.
For he whose soul nought but a soul can move
   Does a new Narcissus prove,
   And his own image love.

   That souls do beauty know
   'Tis to the body's help they owe;
If when they know't they straight abuse that trust
And shut the body from't, 'tis as unjust
As if I brought my dearest friend to see
   My mistress and at th'instant he
   Should steal her quite from me.

## ANNE BRADSTREET

### *To My Dear and Loving Husband*

If ever two were one, then surely we.
If ever man were lov'd by wife, then thee.
If ever wife was happy in a man,
Compare with me, ye women, if you can.
I prise thy love more than whole Mines of gold
Or all the riches that the East doth hold.
My love is such that Rivers cannot quench,
Nor ought but love from thee give recompence.
Thy love is such I can no way repay.
The heavens reward thee manifold, I pray.
Then while we live, in love let's so persever
That when we live no more, we may live ever.


## ROBERT HERRICK

### *Upon Julia's Clothes*

Whenas in silks my Julia goes,
Till, then, methinks, how sweetly flows
That liquefaction of her clothes.

Next, when I cast mine eyes, and see
That brave vibration each way free,
O how that glittering taketh me!

ROBERT HERRICK

## To the Virgins, to Make Much of Time

Gather ye rose-buds while ye may,
    Old Time is still a-flying;
And this same flower that smiles today
    Tomorrow will be dying.

The glorious lamp of heaven, the sun,
    The higher he's a-getting,
The sooner will his race be run,
    And nearer he's to setting.

That age is best which is the first,
    When youth and blood are warmer;
But being spent, the worse, and worst
    Times still succeed the former.

Then be not coy, but use your time,
    And while ye may, go marry:
For having lost but once your prime,
    You may forever tarry.

## Delight in Disorder

A sweet disorder in the dress
Kindles in clothes a wantonness;
A lawn about the shoulders thrown
Into a fine distraction;
An erring lace, which here and there
Enthrals the crimson stomacher;
A cuff neglectful, and thereby
Ribands to flow confusedly;
A winning wave, deserving note,
In the tempestuous petticoat;
A careless shoe-string, in whose tie
I see a wild civility:
Do more bewitch me, than when art
Is too precise in every part.

## JOHN MILTON

### *Sonnet 23*

Methought I saw my late espoused saint
   Brought to me, like Alcestis, from the grave,
   Whom Jove's great son to her glad husband gave,
   Rescued from death by force, though pale and faint.
Mine, as whom washed from spot of childbed taint,
   Purification in the old Law did save,
   And such, as yet once more I trust to have
   Full sight of her in Heaven without restraint,
Came vested all in white, pure as her mind;
   Her face was veiled, yet to my fancied sight
   Love, sweetness, goodness, in her person shined
So clear as in no face with more delight.
   But O! as to embrace me she inclined,
   I waked, she fled, and day brought back my night.

## JOHN MILTON

### FROM *Paradise Lost, Book 4*

That day I oft remember, when from sleep
I first awaked and found myself reposed,
Under a shade of flow'rs, much wond'ring where
And what I was, whence thither brought, and how.
Not distant far from thence a murmuring sound
Of waters issued from a cave, and spread
Into a liquid plain, then stood unmoved,
Pure as th' expanse of heav'n; I thither went
With unexperienced thought, and laid me down
On the green bank, to look into the clear

Smooth lake, that to me seemed another sky.
As I bent down to look, just opposite
A shape within the wat'ry gleam appeared,
Bending to look on me: I started back,
It started back; but pleased I soon returned
Pleased it returned as soon with answering looks
Of sympathy and love; there I had fixed
Mine eyes till now, and pined with vain desire,
Had not a voice thus warned me: 'What thou seest
What there thou seest, fair creature, is thyself:
With thee it came and goes; but follow me,
And I will bring thee where no shadow stays
Thy coming and thy soft embraces, he
Whose image thou art; him thou shalt enjoy
Inseparably thine; to him shalt bear
Multitudes like thyself, and thence be called
Mother of human race.' What could I do
But follow straight, invisibly thus led?
Till I espied thee, fair indeed and tall,
Under a platan; yet methought less fair,
Less winning soft, less amiably mild,
Than that smooth wat'ry image. Back I turn'd;
Thou, following, cried'st aloud, 'Return, fair Eve;
Whom fliest thou? Whom thou fliest, of him thou art,
His flesh, his bone; to give thee being I lent
Out of my side to thee, nearest my heart,
Substantial life, to have thee by my side
Henceforth an individual solace dear:
Part of my soul I seek thee, and thee claim
My other half.' With that thy gentle hand
Seised mine: I yielded, and from that time see
How beauty is excelled by manly grace
And wisdom, which alone is truly fair.

*Love Poetry*

## ANDREW MARVELL

## *To His Coy Mistress*

Had we but world enough, and time,
This coyness, lady, were no crime.
We would sit down and think which way
To walk, and pass our long love's day;
Thou by the Indian Ganges' side
Shouldst rubies find; I by the tide
Of Humber would complain. I would
Love you ten years before the Flood;
And you should, if you please, refuse
Till the conversion of the Jews.
My vegetable love should grow
Vaster than empires, and more slow.
An hundred years should go to praise
Thine eyes, and on thy forehead gaze;
Two hundred to adore each breast,
But thirty thousand to the rest;
An age at least to every part,
And the last age should show your heart.
For, lady, you deserve this state,
Nor would I love at lower rate.

But at my back I always hear
Time's winged chariot hurrying near;
And yonder all before us lie
Deserts of vast eternity.
Thy beauty shall no more be found,
Nor, in thy marble vault, shall sound
My echoing song; then worms shall try
That long preserv'd virginity,
And your quaint honour turn to dust,

And into ashes all my lust.
The grave's a fine and private place,
But none I think do there embrace.

   Now therefore, while the youthful hue
Sits on thy skin like morning dew,
And while thy willing soul transpires
At every pore with instant fires,
Now let us sport us while we may;
And now, like am'rous birds of prey,
Rather at once our time devour,
Than languish in his slow-chapp'd power.
Let us roll all our strength, and all
Our sweetness, up into one ball;
And tear our pleasures with rough strife
Thorough the iron gates of life.
Thus, though we cannot make our sun
Stand still, yet we will make him run.


ANDREW MARVELL

*The Definition of Love*

My love is of a birth as rare
As 'tis for object strange and high;
It was begotten by Despair
Upon Impossibility.

Magnanimous Despair alone
Could show me so divine a thing
Where feeble Hope could ne'er have flown,
But vainly flapp'd its tinsel wing.

And yet I quickly might arrive
Where my extended soul is fixt,
But Fate does iron wedges drive,
And always crowds itself betwixt.

For Fate with jealous eye does see
Two perfect loves, nor lets them close;
Their union would her ruin be,
And her tyrannic power depose.

And therefore her decrees of steel
Us as the distant poles have placed,
(Though love's whole world on us doth wheel)
Not by themselves to be embraced;

Unless the giddy heaven fall,
And earth some new convulsion tear;
And, us to join, the world should all
Be cramped into a planisphere.

As lines, so loves oblique may well
Themselves in every angle greet;
But ours so truly parallel,
Though infinite, can never meet.

Therefore the love which us doth bind,
But Fate so enviously debars,
Is the conjunction of the mind,
And opposition of the stars.

JOHN WILMOT, EARL OF ROCHESTER

## A Song of a Young Lady
## to Her Ancient Lover

Ancient person, for whom I
All the flattering youth defy,
Long be it ere thou grow old,
Aching, shaking, crazy, cold;
    But still continue as thou art,
    Ancient person of my heart.

On thy withered lips and dry,
Which like barren furrows lie,
Brooding kisses I will pour
Shall thy youthful heat restore
(Such kind showers in autumn fall,
And a second spring recall);
    Nor from thee will ever part,
    Ancient person of my heart.

Thy nobler part, which but to name
In our sex would be counted shame,
By age's frozen grasp possessed,
From his ice shall be released,
And soothed by my reviving hand,
In former warmth and vigour stand.
All a lover's wish can reach
For thy joy my love shall teach,
And for they pleasure shall improve
All that art can add to love.
    Yet still I love thee without art,
    Ancient person of my heart.

JOHN WILMOT, EARL OF ROCHESTER

## Love and Life: A Song

All my past life is mine no more;
   The flying hours are gone,
Like transitory dreams given o'er,
Whose images are kept in store
   By memory alone.

The time that is to come is not:
   How can it then be mine?
The present moment's all my lot;
And that, as fast as it is got,
   Phyllis, is wholly thine.

Then talk not of inconstancy,
   False hearts, and broken vows;
If I, by miracle, can be
This live-long minute true to thee,
   'Tis all that Heaven allows.

## *A Song*

Absent from thee, I languish still;
   Then ask me not, when I return?
The straying fool 'twill plainly kill
   To wish all day, all night to mourn.

Dear! from thine arms then let me fly,
   That my fantastic mind may prove
The torments it deserves to try
   That tears my fixed heart from my love.

When, wearied with a world of woe,
   To thy safe bosom I retire
Where love and peace and truth does flow,
   May I contented there expire,

Lest, once more wandering from that heaven,
   I fall on some base heart unblessed,
Faithless to thee, false, unforgiven,
   And lose my everlasting rest.

EDMUND WALLER

## Go, Lovely Rose

Go, lovely rose –
Tell her that wastes her time and me
That now she knows,
When I resemble her to thee,
How sweet and fair she seems to be.

Tell her that's young,
And shuns to have her graces spied,
That hadst thou sprung
In deserts, where no men abide,
Thou must have uncommended died.

Small is the worth
Of beauty from the light retired;
Bid her come forth,
Suffer herself to be desired,
And not blush so to be admired.

Then die – that she
The common fate of all things rare
May read in thee;
How small a part of time they share
That are so wondrous sweet and fair!

JOHN DRYDEN

## Farewell Ungrateful Traitor

Farewell ungrateful traitor,
  Farewell my perjured swain,
Let never injured creature
  Believe a man again.
The pleasure of possessing
Surpasses all expressing,
But 'tis too short a blessing,
  And love too long a pain.

'Tis easy to deceive us
  In pity of your pain,
But when we love you leave us
  To rail at you in vain.
Before we have descried it,
There is no bliss beside it,
But she that once has tried it
  Will never love again.

The passion you pretended
  Was only to obtain,
But when the charm is ended
  The charmer you disdain.
Your love by ours we measure
Till we have lost our treasure,
But dying is a pleasure,
  When living is a pain.

## To Cloris

Cloris, I cannot say your eyes
Did my unwary heart surprise;
Nor will I swear it was your face,
Your shape, or any nameless grace:
For you are so entirely fair,
To love a part, injustice were;
No drowning man can know which drop
Of water his last breath did stop;
So when the stars in heaven appear,
And join to make the night look clear;
The light we no one's bounty call,
But the obliging gift of all.
He that does lips or hands adore,
Deserves them only, and no more;
But I love all, and every part,
And nothing less can ease my heart.
Cupid, that lover, weakly strikes,
Who can express what 'tis he likes.

SIR CHARLES SEDLEY

## Phyllis is My Only Joy

Phyllis is my only joy,
Faithless as the winds or seas;
Sometimes coming, sometimes coy,
Yet she never fails to please;
If with a frown
I am cast down,
Phyllis smiling,
And beguiling,
Makes me happier than before.

Though, alas! too late I find
Nothing can her fancy fix,
Yet the moment she is kind
I forgive her all her tricks;
Which, though I see,
I can't get free;
She deceiving,
I believing;
What need lovers wish for more?

WILLIAM WALSH

## Love and Jealousy

How much are they deceived who vainly strive,
By jealous fears, to keep our flames alive?
Love's like a torch, which if secured from blasts,
Will faintlier burn; but then it longer lasts.
Exposed to storms of jealousy and doubt,
The blaze grows greater, but 'tis sooner out.

## ANNE FINCH, COUNTESS OF WINCHILSEA

### *A Letter to Daphnis*

This to the crown and blessing of my life,
The much loved husband of a happy wife;
To him whose constant passion found the art
To win a stubborn and ungrateful heart,
And to the world by tenderest proof discovers
They err, who say that husbands can't be lovers.
With such return of passion as is due,
Daphnis I love, Daphnis my thoughts pursue;
Daphnis my hopes and joys are bounded all in you.
Even I, for Daphnis' and my promise' sake,
What I in women censure, undertake.
But this from love, not vanity, proceeds;
You know who writes, and I who 'tis that reads.
Judge not my passion by my want of skill:
Many love well, though they express it ill;
And I your censure could with pleasure bear,
Would you but soon return, and speak it here.

**WILLIAM CONGREVE**

### Song

Pious Selinda goes to prayers,
    If I but ask the favour;
And yet the tender fool's in tears,
    When she believes I'll leave her.

Would I were free from this restraint,
    Or else had hopes to win her;
Would she could make of me a saint,
    Or I of her a sinner.


**WILLIAM CONGREVE**

### False Though She be to Me and Love

False though she be to me and love,
    I'll ne'er pursue revenge;
For still the charmer I approve,
    Though I deplore her change.

In hours of bliss we oft have met:
    They could not always last;
And though the present I regret,
    I'm grateful for the past.

## Love

Love is begot by fancy, bred
    By ignorance, by expectation fed,
Destroyed by knowledge, and, at best,
Lost in the moment 'tis possessed.

ALEXANDER POPE

## Epistle to Miss Blount,

### On Her Leaving the Town, after the Coronation

As some fond virgin, whom her mother's care
Drags from the town to wholesome country air,
Just when she learns to roll a melting eye,
And hear a spark, yet think no danger nigh;
From the dear man unwillingly she must sever,
Yet takes one kiss before she parts for ever:
Thus from the world fair Zephalinda flew,
Saw others happy, and with sighs withdrew;
Not that their pleasures caused her discontent,
She sighed not that They stayed, but that She went.
        She went, to plain-work, and to purling brooks,
Old-fashioned halls, dull aunts, and croaking rooks,
She went from Opera, park, assembly, play,
To morning walks, and prayers three hours a day;
To pass her time 'twixt reading and Bohea,
To muse, and spill her solitary tea,
Or o'er cold coffee trifle with the spoon,
Count the slow clock, and dine exact at noon;

Divert her eyes with pictures in the fire,
Hum half a tune, tell stories to the squire;
Up to her godly garret after seven,
There starve and pray, for that's the way to heaven.

Some Squire, perhaps, you take a delight to rack;
Whose game is Whisk, whose treat a toast in sack,
Who visits with a gun, presents you birds,
Then gives a smacking buss, and cries – No words!
Or with his hound comes hollowing from the stable,
Makes love with nods, and knees beneath a table;
Whose laughs are hearty, tho' his jests are coarse,
And loves you best of all things – but his horse.

In some fair evening, on your elbow laid,
Your dream of triumphs in the rural shade;
In pensive thought recall the fancied scene,
See Coronations rise on every green;
Before you pass th' imaginary sights
Of Lords, and Earls, and Dukes, and gartered Knights;
While the spread fan o'ershades your closing eyes;
Then give one flirt, and all the vision flies.
Thus vanish sceptres, coronets, and balls,
And leave you in lone woods, or empty walls.

So when your slave, at some dear, idle time,
(Not plagued with headaches, or the want of rhyme)
Stands in the streets, abstracted from the crew,
And while he seems to study, thinks of you:
Just when his fancy points your sprightly eyes,
Or sees the blush of soft Parthenia rise,
Gay pats my shoulder, and you vanish quite;
Streets, chairs, and coxcombs rush upon my sight;
Vexed to be still in town, I knit my brow,
Look sour, and hum a tune – as you may now.

### ALEXANDER POPE

## *Two or Three: A Recipe to Make a Cuckold*

Two or three visits, and two or three bows,
Two or three civil things, two or three vows,
Two or three kisses, with two or three sighs,
Two or three Jesus's – and let me dies –
Two or three squeezes, and two or three towses,
With two or three thousand pound lost at their houses,
Can never fail cuckolding two or three spouses.

### BENJAMIN FRANKLIN

## *Wedlock*

Wedlock as old men note, hath likened been,
Unto a public crowd or common rout;
Where those that are without would fain get in,
And those that are within, would fain get out.
Grief often treads upon the heels of pleasure,
Marry'd in haste, we oft repent at leisure;
Some by experience find these words missplaced,
Marry'd at leisure, they repent in haste.

ROBERT BURNS

## A Red, Red Rose

O my Luve's like a red, red rose
   That's newly sprung in June;
O my Luve's like the melodie
   That's sweetly play'd in tune. –

As fair art thou, my bonie lass,
   So deep in luve am I;
And I will luve thee still, my dear,
   Till a' the seas gang dry. –

Till a' the seas gang dry, my dear,
   And the rocks melt wi' the sun:
I will luve thee still, my dear,
   While the sands o' life shall run. –

And fare thee well, my only Luve!
   And fare thee well, a while!
And I will come again, my Luve,
   Tho' it were ten thousand mile!

## ROBERT BURNS

### *The Banks o' Doon*

Ye flowery banks o' bonie Doon,
　How can ye blume sae fair;
How can ye chant, ye little birds,
　And I sae fu' o' care!

Thou'll break my heart, thou bonie bird
　That sings upon the bough;
Thou minds me o' the happy days
　When my fause luve was true.

Thou'll break my heart, thou bonie bird
　That sings beside thy mate;
For sae I sat, and sae I sang,
　And wist na o' my fate.

Aft hae I rov'd by bonie Doon,
　To see the woodbine twine,
And ilka bird sang o' its love,
　And sae did I o' mine.

Wi' lightsome heart I pu'd a rose
　Frae aff its thorny tree,
And my fause luver staw the rose,
　But left the thorn wi' me.

Wi' lightsome heart I pu'd a rose,
　Upon a morn in June:
And sae I flourish'd on the morn,
　And sae was pu'd or noon!

## ROBERT BURNS

### *Corn Rigs*

It was upon a Lammas night,
　　When corn rigs are bonie,
Beneath the moon's unclouded light,
　　I held awa to Annie:
The time flew by, wi' tentless heed,
　　Till 'tween the late and early;
Wi' sma' persuasion she agreed,
　　To see me thro' the barley.

*Chorus*
Corn rigs, an' barley rigs,
An' corn rigs are bonie:
I'll ne'er forget that happy night,
Amang the rigs wi' Annie.

The sky was blue, the wind was still,
　　The moon was shining clearly;
I set her down, wi' right good will,
　　Amang the rigs o' barley:
I ken't her heart was a' my ain;
　　I lov'd her most sincerely;
I kiss'd her owre and owre again,
　　Amang the rigs o' barley.

I lock'd her in my fond embrace;
　　Her heart was beating rarely:
My blessings on that happy place,
　　Amang the rigs o' barley!
But by the moon and stars so bright,
　　That shone that hour so clearly!

She ay shall bless that happy night
   Amang the rigs o' barley.

I hae been blythe wi' Comrades dear;
   I hae been merry drinking;
I hae been joyfu' gath'rin gear;
   I hae been happy thinking:
But a' the pleasures e'er I saw,
   Tho' three times doubl'd fairly,
That happy night was worth them a',
   Amang the rigs o' barley.

ROBERT BURNS

## John Anderson My Jo

John Anderson my jo, John,
   When we were first acquent,
Your locks were like the raven,
   Your bonie brow was brent;
But now your brow is beld, John,
   Your locks are like the snaw,
but blessings on your frosty pow,
   John Anderson my jo!

John Anderson my jo, John,
   We clamb the hill thegither,
And monie a cantie day, John,
   We've had wi' ane anither;
Now we maun totter down, John,
   And hand in hand we'll go,
And sleep thegither at the foot,
   John Anderson, my jo!

## JOHN KEATS

### *Ode to a Nightingale*

My heart aches, and a drowsy numbness pains
    My sense, as though of hemlock I had drunk,
Or emptied some dull opiate to the drains
    One minute past, and Lethe-wards had sunk:
'Tis not through envy of thy happy lot,
    But being too happy in thine happiness, –
        That thou, light-winged Dryad of the trees
          In some melodious plot
Of beechen green, and shadows numberless,
    Singest of summer in full-throated ease.

O, for a draught of vintage! that hath been
    Cool'd a long age in the deep-delved earth,
Tasting of Flora and the country green,
    Dance, and Provençal song, and sunburnt mirth!
O for a beaker full of the warm South,
    Full of the true, the blushful Hippocrene,
        With beaded bubbles winking at the brim,
          And purple-stained mouth;
That I might drink, and leave the world unseen,
    And with thee fade away into the forest dim:

Fade far away, dissolve, and quite forget
    What thou among the leaves hast never known,
The weariness, the fever, and the fret
    Here, where men sit and hear each other groan;
Where palsy shakes a few, sad, last gray hairs,
    Where youth grows pale, and spectre-thin,
                    and dies;
    Where but to think is to be full of sorrow

                    And leaden-eyed despairs,
            Where Beauty cannot keep her lustrous eyes,
                Or new Love pine at them beyond tomorrow

Away! away! for I will fly to thee,
            Not charioted by Bacchus and his pards,
But on the viewless wings of Poesy,
            Though the dull brain perplexes and retards:
Already with thee! tender is the night,
            And haply the Queen-Moon is on her throne,
                Cluster'd around by all her starry Fays;
                    But here there is no light,
            Save what from heaven is with the breezes blown
                Through verdurous glooms and winding
                                              mossy ways.

I cannot see what flowers are at my feet,
            Nor what soft incense hangs upon the boughs,
But, in embalmed darkness, guess each sweet
            Wherewith the seasonable month endows
The grass, the thicket, and the fruit-tree wild;
            White hawthorn, and the pastoral eglantine;
                Fast fading violets cover'd up in leaves;
                    And mid-May's eldest child,
            The coming musk-rose, full of dewy wine,
                The murmurous haunt of flies on summer eves.

Darkling I listen; and, for many a time
            I have been half in love with easeful Death,
Call'd him soft names in many a mused rhyme,
            To take into the air my quiet breath;
                Now more than ever seems it rich to die,
            To cease upon the midnight with no pain,
                While thou art pouring forth thy soul abroad
                    In such an ecstasy!

Still wouldst thou sing, and I have ears in vain –
　　To thy high requiem become a sod.

Thou wast not born for death, immortal Bird!
　　No hungry generations tread thee down;
The voice I hear this passing night was heard
　　In ancient days by emperor and clown:
Perhaps the self-same song that found a path
　　Through the sad heart of Ruth, when,
　　　　　　　　　sick for home,
　　　She stood in tears amid the alien corn;
　　　　The same that oft-times hath
　　Charm'd magic casements, opening on the foam
　　Of perilous seas, in faery lands forlorn.

Forlorn! the very word is like a bell
　　To toll me back from thee to my sole self!
Adieu! the fancy cannot cheat so well
　　As she is fam'd to do, deceiving elf.
Adieu! adieu! thy plaintive anthem fades
　　Past the near meadows, over the still stream,
　　　Up the hillside; and now 'tis buried deep
　　　In the next valley-glades:
　　Was it a vision, or a waking dream?
　　　Fled is that music: – Do I wake or sleep?

JOHN KEATS

## Bright Star

Bright star, would I were stedfast as thou art –
Not in lone splendour hung aloft the night
And watching, with eternal lids apart,
Like nature's patient, sleepless Eremite,
The moving waters at their priestlike task
Of pure ablution round earth's human shores,
Or gazing on the new soft-fallen mask
Of snow upon the mountains and the moors –
No–yet still stedfast, still unchangeable,
Pillow'd upon my fair love's ripening breast,
To feel for ever its soft fall and swell,
Awake for ever in a sweet unrest,
    Still, still to hear her tender-taken breath,
    And so live ever – or else swoon to death.

## *To Fanny*

I cry your mercy – pity – love! – aye, love!
    Merciful love that tantalises not,
One-thoughted, never-wandering, guileless love,
    Unmasked, and being seen – without a blot!
O! let me have thee whole, – all – all – be mine!
    That shape, that fairness, that sweet minor zest
Of love, your kiss, – those hands, those eyes divine,
    That warm, white, lucent, million-
                                        pleasured breast, –
Yourself – your soul – in pity give me all,
    Withhold no atom's atom or I die
Or living on perhaps, your wretched thrall,
    Forget, in the mist of idle misery,
Life's purposes, – the palate of my mind
Losing its gust, and my ambition blind!

## La Belle Dame Sans Merci: A Ballad

Oh what can ail thee, knight-at-arms,
    Alone and palely loitering?
The sedge has withered from the lake,
    And no birds sing.

Oh what can ail thee, knight-at-arms,
    So haggard and so woebegone?
The squirrel's granary is full,
    And the harvest's done.

I see a lily on thy brow,
    With anguish moist and fever-dew,
And on thy cheeks a fading rose
    Fast withereth too.

I met a lady in the meads,
    Full beautiful – a faery's child,
Her hair was long, her foot was light,
    And her eyes were wild.

I made a garland for her head,
    And bracelets too, and fragrant zone;
She looked at me as she did love,
    And made sweet moan.

I set her on my pacing steed,
    And nothing else saw all day long,
For sidelong would she bend, and sing
    A faery's song.

She found me roots of relish sweet,
    And honey wild, and manna-dew,
And sure in language strange she said –
    'I love thee true'.

She took me to her elfin grot,
    And there she wept and sighed full sore,

And there I shut her wild wild eyes
　　With kisses four.
And there she lulled me asleep
　　And there I dreamed – Ah! woe betide! –
The latest dream I ever dreamt
　　On the cold hill side.
I saw pale kings and princes too,
　　Pale warriors, death-pale were they all;
They cried – 'La Belle Dame sans Merci
　　Hath thee in thrall!'
I saw their starved lips in the gloam,
　　With horrid warning gaped wide,
And I awoke and found me here,
　　On the cold hill's side.
And this is why I sojourn here
　　Alone and palely loitering,
Though the sedge is withered from the lake,
　　And no birds sing.

PERCY BYSSHE SHELLEY

## Love's Philosophy

The fountains mingle with the river,
   And the rivers with the ocean;
The winds of heaven mix forever,
   With a sweet emotion;
Nothing in the world is single;
   All things by a law divine
In one another's being mingle; –
   Why not I with thine?

See! the mountains kiss high heaven,
   And the waves clasp one another;
No sister flower would be forgiven,
   If it disdained it's brother;
And the sunlight clasps the earth,
   And the moonbeams kiss the sea; –
What are all these kissings worth,
   If thou kiss not me?

PERCY BYSSHE SHELLEY

## Art Thou Pale for Weariness

Art thou pale for weariness
Of climbing heaven and gazing on the earth,
   Wandering companionless
Among the stars that have a different birth,
And ever changing, like a joyless eye
That finds no object worth its constancy?

## *To Jane: The Invitation*

Best and brightest, come away!
Fairer far than this fair Day,
Which, like thee to those in sorrow,
Comes to bid a sweet good-morrow
To the rough Year just awake
In its cradle on the brake.
The Brightest hour of unborn Spring,
Through the winter wandering,
Found, it seems, the halcyon Morn
To hoar February born.
Bending from Heaven, in azure mirth,
It kissed the forehead of the Earth,
And smiled upon the silent sea,
And bade the frozen streams be free,
And waked to music all their fountains,
And breathed upon the frozen mountains,
And like a prophetess of May
Strewed flowers upon the barren way,
Making the wintry world appear
Like one on whom thou smilest, dear.

Away, away, from men and towns,
To the wild wood and the downs –
To the silent wilderness
Where the soul need not repress
Its music lest it should not find
An echo in another's mind.
While the touch of Nature's art
Harmonises heart to heart.
I leave this notice on my door

For each accustomed visitor: –
'I am gone into the fields
To take what this sweet hour yields; –
Reflection, you may come tomorrow,
Sit by the fireside with Sorrow. –
You with the unpaid bill, Despair, –
You, tiresome verse-reciter, Care, –
I will pay you in the grave, –
Death will listen to your stave.
Expectation too, be off!
Today is for itself enough;
Hope, in pity mock not Woe
With smiles, nor follow where I go;
Long having lived on thy sweet food,
At length I find one moment's good
After long pain – with all your love,
This you never told me of.'

Radiant Sister of the Day,
Awake! Arise! And come away!
To the wild woods and the plains,
And the pools where winter rains
Image all their roof of leaves,
Where the pine its garland weaves
Of sapless green, and ivy dun
Round stems that never kiss the sun:
Where the lawns and pastures be,
And the sandhills of the sea: –
Where the melting hoar-frost wets
The daisy-star that never sets,
And wind-flowers, and violets,
Which yet join not scent to hue,
Crown the pale year weak and new;
When the night is left behind
In the deep east, dun and blind,

And the blue noon is over us,
And the multitudinous
Billows murmur at our feet,
Where the earth and ocean meet,
And all things seem only one
In the universal sun.


PERCY BYSSHE SHELLEY

## *To Jane*

### I

The keen stars were twinkling,
And the fair moon was rising among them,
Dear Jane.
The guitar was tinkling,
But the notes were not sweet till you sung them
Again.

### 2

As the moon's soft splendour
O'er the faint cold starlight of Heaven
Is thrown,
So your voice most tender
To the strings without soul had then given
Its own.

### 3

The stars will awaken,
Though the moon sleep a full hour later,
Tonight;
No leaf will be shaken
Whilst the dews of your melody scatter
Delight.

Though the sound overpowers,
Sing again, with your dear voice revealing
A tone
Of some world far from ours,
Where music and moonlight and feeling
Are one.


PERCY BYSSHE SHELLEY

*Music*

Music, when soft voices die,
Vibrates in the memory –
Odours, when sweet violets sicken,
Live within the sense they quicken.

Rose leaves, when the rose is dead,
Are heaped for the belovèd's bed;
And so thy thoughts, when thou art gone,
Love itself shall slumber on.

### LORD BYRON

## *She Walks in Beauty*

She walks in beauty, like the night
   Of cloudless climes and starry skies;
And all that's best of dark and bright
   Meet in her aspect and her eyes;
Thus mellowed to that tender light
   Which heaven to gaudy day denies.

One shade the more, one ray the less,
   Had half impaired the nameless grace
Which waves in every raven tress,
   Or softly lightens o'er her face;
Where thoughts serenely sweet express,
   How pure, how dear their dwelling-place.

And on that cheek, and o'er that brow,
   So soft, so calm, yet eloquent,
The smiles that win, the tints that glow,
   But tell of days in goodness spent,
A mind at peace with all below,
   A heart whose love is innocent!

LORD BYRON

## Love and Death

I watched thee when the foe was at our side,
　　Ready to strike at him, or thee and me,
Were safety hopeless rather than divide
　　Aught with one loved save love and liberty.

I watched thee on the breakers, when the rock,
　　Received our prow, and all was storm and fear,
And bade thee cling to me through every shock;
　　This arm would be thy bark, or breast thy bier.

I watched thee when the fever glazed thine eyes,
　　Yielding my couch and stretched me on the ground
When overworn with watching, ne'er to rise
　　From thence if thou an early grave hadst found.

The earthquake came, and rocked the quivering wall,
　　And men and nature reeled as if with wine.
Whom did I seek around the tottering hall
　　For thee, whose safety first provide for thine.

And when convulsive throes denied my breath
　　The faintest utterance to my fading thought,
To thee, to thee, even in the grasp of death
　　My spirit turned. Ah! oftener than it ought.

Thus much and more; and yet thou lov'st me not,
　　And never wilt! Love dwells not in our will.
Nor can I blame thee, though it be my lot
　　To strongly, wrongly, vainly love thee still.

*Love Poetry*

## LORD BYRON

### *When We Two Parted*

When we two parted
   In silence and tears,
Half broken-hearted
   To sever for years,
Pale grew thy cheek and cold,
   Colder thy kiss;
Truly that hour foretold
   Sorrow to this.

The dew of the morning
   Sunk chill on my brow –
It felt like the warning
   Of what I feel now.
Thy vows are all broken,
   And light is thy fame;
I hear thy name spoken,
   And share in its shame.

They name thee before me,
   A knell to mine ear;
A shudder comes o'er me –
   Why wert thou so dear?
They know not I knew thee,
   Who knew thee too well –
Long, long shall I rue thee,
   Too deeply to tell.

In secret we met –
   In silence I grieve,
That thy heart could forget,
   Thy spirit deceive.

If I should meet thee
   After long years,
How should I greet thee?
   With silence and tears.

LORD BYRON

## So, We'll Go No More A-Roving

So, we'll go no more a-roving
   So late into the night,
Though the heart be still as loving,
   And the moon be still as bright.

For the sword outwears its sheath,
   And the soul wears out the breast,
And the heart must pause to breathe,
   And love itself have rest.

Though the night was made for loving,
   And the day returns too soon,
Yet we'll go no more a-roving
   By the light of the moon.

## LORD BYRON

### *Remember Thee!*

Remember thee! Remember thee!
   Till Lethe quench life's burning stream
Remorse and shame shall cling to thee,
   And haunt thee like a feverish dream!

Remember thee! Aye, doubt it not.
   Thy husband too shall think of thee:
By neither shalt thou be forgot,
   Thou *false* to him, thou *fiend* to me!

WILLIAM BLAKE

*Love's Secret*

Never seek to tell thy love,
Love that never told can be;
For the gentle wind doth move
Silently, invisibly.

I told my love, I told my love,
I told her all my heart,
Trembling, cold, in ghastly fears.
Ah! she did depart!

Soon after she was gone from me,
A traveller came by,
Silently, invisibly:
O, was no deny.

WILLIAM BLAKE

*The Sick Rose*

O Rose thou art sick.
The invisible worm,
That flies in the night
In the howling storm:

Has found out thy bed
Of crimson joy:
And his dark secret love
Does thy life destroy.

### WILLIAM BLAKE

## The Clod and the Pebble

'Love seeketh not itself to please,
Nor for itself hath any care,
But for another gives its ease,
And builds a Heaven in Hell's despair.'

So sung a little Clod of Clay
Trodden with the cattle's feet,
But a Pebble of the brook
Warbled out these metres meet:

'Love seeketh only self to please,
To bind another to its delight,
Joys in another's loss of ease,
And builds a Hell in Heaven's despite.'

### GEORGE CRABBE

## A Marriage Ring

The ring, so worn as you behold,
So thin, so pale, is yet of gold:
The passion such it was to prove –
Worn with life's cares, love yet was love.

## Rover

'A weary lot is thine, fair maid,
A weary lot is thine!
To pull the thorn thy brow to braid,
And press the rue for wine.
A lightsome eye, a soldier's mien,
A feather of the blue,
A doublet of the Lincoln green –
No more of me you knew,
My love!
No more of me you knew.'

'The morn is merry June, I trow,
The rose is budding fain;
But she shall bloom in winter snow
Ere we two meet again.'
He turn'd his charger as he spake
Upon the river shore,
He gave the bridle-reins a shake,
Said, 'Adieu for evermore,
My love!
And adieu for evermore.'

## Where shall the Lover Rest

Where shall the lover rest,
Whom the fates sever
From his true maiden's breast,
Parted for ever?
Where, through groves deep and high,
Sounds the far billow,
Where early violets die,
Under the willow.
*Eleu loro*
*Soft shall be his pillow.*

There, through the summer day,
Cool streams are laving;
There, while the tempests sway,
Scarce are boughs waving;
There, thy rest shalt thou take,
Parted for ever,
Never again to wake,
Never, O never!
*Eleu loro*
*Never, O never!*

Where shall the traitor rest,
He the deceiver,
Who could win maiden's breast,
Ruin, and leave her?
In the lost battle,
Borne down by the flying,
Where ingles wars rattle,
With groans of the dying;
*Eleu loro*
*There shall he be lying*

Her wing shall the eagle flap,
O'er the falsehearted,
This warm blood the wolf shall lap,
Ere life be parted.
Shame and dishonour sit
By his grave ever,
Blessing shall hallow it
Never, O never !
*Eleu loro*
*Never, O never!*

### SIR WALTER SCOTT

## *An Hour with Thee*

An hour with thee! When earliest day
Dapples with gold the eastern grey,
Oh, what can frame my mind to bear
The toil and turmoil, cark and care,
New griefs, which coming hours unfold,
And sad remembrance of the old?
       One hour with thee.

One hour with thee! When burning June
Waves his red flag at pitch of noon;
What shall repay the faithful swain,
His labour on the sultry plain;
And, more than cave or sheltering bough,
Cool feverish blood and throbbing brow?
       One hour with thee.

One hour with thee! When sun is set,
Oh, what can teach me to forget
The thankless labours of the day;
The hopes, the wishes, flung away;
The increasing wants, and lessening gains,
The master's pride, who scorns my pains?
       One hour with thee.

## Love

All thoughts, all passions, all delights,
Whatever stirs this mortal frame,
All are but ministers of Love,
    And feed his sacred flame.

Oft in my waking dreams do I
Live o'er again that happy hour,
When midway on the mount I lay,
    Beside the ruined tower.

The moonshine, stealing o'er the scene
Had blended with the lights of eve;
And she was there, my hope, my joy,
    My own dear Genevieve!

She leant against the armèd man,
The statue of the armèd knight;
She stood and listened to my lay,
    Amid the lingering light.

Few sorrows hath she of her own,
My hope! my joy! my Genevieve!
She loves me best, whene'er I sing
    The songs that make her grieve.

I played a soft and doleful air,
I sang an old and moving story –
An old rude song, that suited well
    That ruin wild and hoary.

She listened with a flitting blush,
With downcast eyes and modest grace;
For well she knew, I could not choose
But gaze upon her face.

I told her of the Knight that wore
Upon his shield a burning brand;
And that for ten long years he wooed
The Lady of the Land.

I told her how he pined: and ah!
The deep, the low, the pleading tone
With which I sang another's love,
Interpreted my own.

She listened with a flitting blush,
With downcast eyes, and modest grace;
And she forgave me, that I gazed
Too fondly on her face!

But when I told the cruel scorn
That crazed that bold and lovely Knight,
And that he crossed the mountain-woods,
Nor rested day nor night;

That sometimes from the savage den,
And sometimes from the darksome shade,
And sometimes starting up at once
In green and sunny glade, –

There came and looked him in the face
An angel beautiful and bright;
And that he knew it was a Fiend,
This miserable Knight!

And that unknowing what he did,
He leaped amid a murderous band,
And saved from outrage worse than death
    The Lady of the Land!

And how she wept, and clasped his knees;
And how she tended him in vain –
And ever strove to expiate
    The scorn that crazed his brain; –

And that she nursed him in a cave;
And how his madness went away,
When on the yellow forest-leaves
    A dying man he lay; –

His dying words – but when I reached
That tenderest strain of all the ditty,
My faltering voice and pausing harp
    Disturbed her soul with pity!

All impulses of soul and sense
Had thrilled my guileless Genevieve;
The music and the doleful tale,
    The rich and balmy eve;

And hopes, and fears that kindle hope,
An undistinguishable throng,
And gentle wishes long subdued,
    Subdued and cherished long!

She wept with pity and delight,
She blushed with love, and virgin-shame;
And like the murmur of a dream,
    I heard her breathe my name.

          *Love Poetry*

Her bosom heaved – she stepped aside,
As conscious of my look she stepped –
Then suddenly, with timorous eye
    She fled to me and wept.

She half enclosed me with her arms,
She pressed me with a meek embrace;
And bending back her head, looked up,
    And gazed upon my face.

'Twas partly love, and partly fear,
And partly 'twas a bashful art,
That I might rather feel, than see,
    The swelling of her heart.

I calmed her fears, and she was calm,
And told her love with virgin pride;
And so I won my Genevieve,
    My bright and beauteous Bride.

## SAMUEL TAYLOR COLERIDGE

### Desire

Where true Love burns Desire is Love's pure flame;
It is the reflex of our earthly frame,
That takes its meaning from the nobler part,
And but translates the language of the heart.


## SAMUEL TAYLOR COLERIDGE

### The Presence of Love

And in Life's noisiest hour,
There whispers still the ceaseless Love of Thee,
The heart's Self-solace and soliloquy.

You mould my Hopes, you fashion me within;
And to the leading Love-throb in the Heart
Thro' all my Being, thro' my pulse's beat;
You lie in all my many Thoughts, like Light,
Like the fair light of Dawn, or summer Eve
On rippling Stream, or cloud-reflecting Lake.

And looking to the Heaven, that bends above you,
How oft! I bless the Lot that made me love you.

## Remembrance

Cold in the earth – and the deep snow piled above thee,
Far, far removed, cold in the dreary grave!
Have I forgot, my only Love, to love thee,
Severed at last by Time's all-severing wave?

Now, when alone, do my thoughts no longer hover
Over the mountains, on that northern shore,
Resting their wings where heath and fern-leaves cover
Thy noble heart forever, ever more?

Cold in the earth – and fifteen wild Decembers,
From those brown hills, have melted into spring:
Faithful, indeed, is the spirit that remembers
After such years of change and suffering!

Sweet Love of youth, forgive, if I forget thee,
While the world's tide is bearing me along;
Other desires and other hopes beset me,
Hopes which obscure, but cannot do thee wrong!

No later light has lightened up my heaven,
No second morn has ever shone for me;
All my life's bliss from thy dear life was given,
All my life's bliss is in the grave with thee.

But, when the days of golden dreams had perished,
And even Despair was powerless to destroy,
Then did I learn how existence could be cherished,
Strengthened, and fed without the aid of joy.

Then did I check the tears of useless passion –
Weaned my young soul from yearning after thine;
Sternly denied its burning wish to hasten
Down to that tomb already more than mine.

And, even yet, I dare not let it languish,
Dare not indulge in memory's rapturous pain;
Once drinking deep of that divinest anguish,
How could I seek the empty world again?


EMILY BRONTË

## Love and Friendship

Love is like the wild rose-briar,
Friendship like the holly-tree –
The holly is dark when the rose-briar blooms
But which will bloom most constantly?

The wild rose-briar is sweet in spring,
Its summer blossoms scent the air;
Yet wait till winter comes again
And who will call the wild-briar fair?

Then scorn the silly rose-wreath now
And deck thee with the holly's sheen,
That when December blights thy brow
He still may leave thy garland green.

EDGAR ALLAN POE

## To Helen

Helen, thy beauty is to me
   Like those Nicean barks of yore
That gently, o'er a perfumed sea,
   The weary, way-worn wanderer bore
   To his own native shore.

On desperate seas long wont to roam,
   Thy hyacinth hair, thy classic face,
Thy Naiad airs have brought me home
   To the glory that was Greece,
   To the grandeur that was Rome.

Lo! in yon brilliant window-niche
   How statue-like I see thee stand,
   The agate lamp within thy hand!
Ah, Psyche, from the regions which
   Are Holy Land!

## Annabel Lee

It was many and many a year ago,
    In a kingdom by the sea,
That a maiden there lived whom you may know
    By the name of Annabel Lee;
And this maiden she lived with no other thought
    Than to love and be loved by me.

I was a child and she was a child,
    In this kingdom by the sea,
But we loved with a love that was more than love –
    I and my Annabel Lee –
With a love that the wingèd seraphs of Heaven
    Coveted her and me.

And this was the reason that, long ago,
    In this kingdom by the sea,
A wind blew out of a cloud, chilling
    My beautiful Annabel Lee;
So that her highborn kinsmen came
    And bore her away from me,
To shut her up in a sepulchre
    In this kingdom by the sea.

The angels, not half so happy in Heaven,
    Went envying her and me –
Yes! – that was the reason (as all men know,
    In this kingdom by the sea)
That the wind came out of the cloud by night,
    Chilling and killing my Annabel Lee.

But our love it was stronger by far than the love
  Of those who were older than we –
  Of many far wiser than we –
And neither the angels in Heaven above
  Nor the demons down under the sea
Can ever dissever my soul from the soul
  Of the beautiful Annabel Lee;

For the moon never beams, without bringing
                                    me dreams
  Of the beautiful Annabel Lee;
And the stars never rise, but I feel the bright eyes
  Of the beautiful Annabel Lee;
And so, all the night-tide, I lie down by the side
  Of my darling – my darling – my life and my bride,
  In her sepulchre there by the sea –
  In her tomb by the sounding sea.

### WILLIAM WORDSWORTH

## *She Dwelt Among the Untrodden Ways*

She dwelt among the untrodden ways
   Beside the springs of Dove,
A Maid whom there were none to praise
   And very few to love:

A violet by a mossy stone
   Half hidden from the eye!
– Fair as a star, when only one
   Is shining in the sky.

She lived unknown, and few could know
   When Lucy ceased to be;
But she is in her grave, and, oh,
   The difference to me!

## Surprised by Joy

Surprised by joy – impatient as the Wind
   I turned to share the transport – Oh! with whom
   But Thee, long buried in the silent tomb,
That spot which no vicissitude can find?
Love, faithful love, recalled thee to my mind –
   But how could I forget thee? – Through what power,
   Even for the least division of an hour,
Have I been so beguiled as to be blind
To my most grievous loss! – That thought's return
   Was the worst pang that sorrow ever bore,
Save one, one only, when I stood forlorn,
   Knowing my heart's best treasure was no more;
That neither present time, nor years unborn
   Could to my sight that heavenly face restore.

## WILLIAM WORDSWORTH

### *A Complaint*

There is a change – and I am poor;
Your love hath been, nor long ago,
A fountain at my fond heart's door,
Whose only business was to flow;
And flow it did; not taking heed
Of its own bounty, or my need.

What happy moments did I count!
Blessed was I then all bliss above!
Now, for that consecrated fount
Of murmuring, sparkling, living love,
What have I? Shall I dare to tell?
A comfortless and hidden well.

A well of love – it may be deep –
I trust it is, – and never dry:
What matter? If the waters sleep
In silence and obscurity.
– Such change, and at the very door
Of my fond heart, hath made me poor.

THOMAS MOORE

## *Believe Me*

Believe me, if all those endearing young charms,
Which I gaze on so fondly today,
Were to change by tomorrow and fleet in my arms,
Like fairy gifts fading away,
Thou wouldst still be adored, as this moment thou art,
Let thy loveliness fade as it will;
And around the dear ruin each wish of my heart
Would entwine itself verdantly still.

It is not while beauty and youth are thine own,
And thy cheeks unprofaned by a tear,
That the fervour and faith of a soul can be known,
To which time will but make thee more dear.
No, the heart that has truly loved never forgets,
But as truly loves on to the close:
As the sunflower turns on her god when he sets
The same look which she turned when he rose.

THOMAS MOORE

## *She is Far from the Land*

She is far from the land, where her young hero sleeps,
And lovers are round her, sighing;
But coldly she turns from their gaze, and weeps,
For her heart in his grave is lying!

She sings the wild song of her dear native plains,
Every note which he loved awaking –
Ah! little they think, who delight in her strains,
How the heart of the minstrel is breaking!

He had loved for his love, for his country he died,
They were all that to life had entwin'd him, –
Nor soon shall the tears of his country be dried,
Nor long will his love stay behind him.

Oh! make her a grave, where the sunbeams rest,
When they promise a glorious morrow;
They'll shine o'er her sleep, like a smile from the West,
From her own loved Island of sorrow!

THOMAS MOORE

### *An Argument*

I've oft been told by learned friars,
    That wishing and the crime are one,
And Heaven punishes desires
    As much as if the deed were done.

If wishing damns us, you and I
    Are damned to all our heart's content;
Come, then, at least we may enjoy
    Some pleasure for our punishment!

THOMAS MOORE

## *Did Not*

'Twas a new feeling – something more
Than we had dared to own before,
   Which then we hid not;
We saw it in each other's eye,
And wished, in every half-breathed sigh,
   To speak, but did not.

She felt my lips' impassioned touch –
'Twas the first time I dared so much,
   And yet she chid not;
But whispered o'er my burning brow,
'Oh, do you doubt I love you now?'
   Sweet soul! I did not.

Warmly I felt her bosom thrill,
I pressed it closer, closer still,
   Though gently bid not;
Till – oh! the world hath seldom heard
Of lovers, who so nearly erred,
   And yet, who did not.

## Jenny Kiss'd Me

Jenny kiss'd me when we met,
   Jumping from the chair she sat in;
Time, you thief, who love to get
   Sweets into your list, put that in!
Say I'm weary, say I'm sad,
   Say that health and wealth have miss'd me,
Say I'm growing old, but add,
   Jenny kiss'd me.

ELIZABETH BARRETT BROWNING

## Sonnet 14

from *Sonnets from the Portuguese*

If thou must love me, let it be for nought
Except for love's sake only. Do not say
'I love her for her smile . . . her look . . . her way
Of speaking gently . . . for a trick of thought
That falls in well with mine, and certes brought
A sense of pleasant ease on such a day' –
For these things in themselves, Beloved, may
Be changed, or change for thee – and love, so wrought,
May be unwrought so. Neither love me for
Thine own dear pity's wiping my cheeks dry, –
A creature might forget to weep, who bore
Thy comfort long, and lose thy love thereby!
But love me for love's sake, that evermore
Thou mayst love on, through love's eternity.

## *Sonnet 38*

from *Sonnets from the Portuguese*

First time he kissed me, he but only kissed
The fingers of this hand wherewith I write,
And ever since it grew more clean and white, . . .
Slow to world-greetings, quick with its 'Oh, list,'
When the angels speak. A ring of amethyst
I could not wear here plainer to my sight,
Than that first kiss. The second passed in height
The first, and sought the forehead, and half missed,
Half falling on the hair. O beyond meed!
That was the chrism of love, which love's own crown,
With sanctifying sweetness, did precede.
The third, upon my lips, was folded down
In perfect, purple state! since when, indeed,
I have been proud and said, 'My Love, my own.'

## Sonnet 43

from *Sonnets from the Portuguese*

How do I love thee? Let me count the ways.
I love thee to the depth and breadth and height
My soul can reach, when feeling out of sight
For the ends of being and ideal grace.
I love thee to the level of every day's
Most quiet need, by sun and candle-light.
I love thee freely, as men strive for right;
I love thee purely, as they turn from praise.
I love thee with the passion put to use
In my old griefs, and with my childhood's faith.
I love thee with a love I seemed to lose
With my lost saints. I love thee with the breath,
Smiles, tears, of all my life; and, if God choose,
I shall but love thee better after death.

JOHN CLARE

## First Love

I ne'er was struck before that hour
    With love so sudden and so sweet,
Her face it bloomed like a sweet flower
    And stole my heart away complete.
My face turned pale as deadly pale,
    My legs refused to walk away,
And when she looked, what could I ail?
    My life and all seemed turned to clay.

And then my blood rushed to my face
    And took my eyesight quite away,
The trees and bushes round the place
    Seemed midnight at noonday.
I could not see a single thing,
    Words from my eyes did start –
They spoke as chords do from the string,
    And blood burnt round my heart.

Are flowers the winter's choice?
    Is love's bed always snow?
She seemed to hear my silent voice,
    Not love's appeals to know.
I never saw so sweet a face
    As that I stood before.
My heart has left its dwelling-place
    And can return no more.

## I Hid my Love when Young

I hid my love when young till I
Couldn't bear the buzzing of a fly;
I hid my love to my despite
Till I could not bear to look at light:
I dare not gaze upon her face
But left her memory in each place;
Where'er I saw a wild flower lie
I kissed and bade my love goodbye.

I met her in the greenest dells,
Where dewdrops pearl the wood bluebells;
The lost breeze kissed her bright blue eye,
The bee kissed and went singing by,
A sunbeam found a passage there,
A gold chain round her neck so fair;
As secret as the wild bee's song
She lay there all the summer long.

I hid my love in field and town
Till e'en the breeze would knock me down;
The bees seemed singing ballads o'er,
The fly's bass turned a lion's roar;
And even silence found a tongue,
To haunt me all the summer long;
The riddle nature could not prove
Was nothing else but secret love.

JOHN CLARE

## The Secret

I loved thee, though I told thee not,
    Right earlily and long,
Thou wert my joy in every spot,
    My theme in every song.

And when I saw a stranger face
    Where beauty held the claim,
I gave it like a secret grace
    The being of thy name.

And all the charms of face or voice
    Which I in others see
Are but the recollected choice
    Of what I felt for thee.

## *To Mary*

I sleep with thee, and wake with thee,
And yet thou art not there;
I fill my arms with thoughts of thee,
And press the common air.
Thy eyes are gazing upon mine,
When thou art out of sight;
My lips are always touching thine,
At morning, noon, and night.

I think and speak of other things
To keep my mind at rest:
But still to thee my memory clings
Like love in woman's breast.
I hide it from the world's wide eye,
And think and speak contrary;
But soft the wind comes from the sky,
And whispers tales of Mary.

The night wind whispers in my ear,
The moons shines in my face;
A burden still of chilling fear
I find in every place.
The breeze is whispering in the bush,
And the dews fall from the tree,
All sighing on, and will not hush,
Some pleasant tales of thee.

## WALTER SAVAGE LANDOR

### *You Smiled, You Spoke, and I Believed*

You smiled, you spoke, and I believed,
By every word and smile deceived.
Another man would hope no more;
Nor hope I what I hoped before:
But let not this last wish be vain;
Deceive, deceive me once again!


## WALTER SAVAGE LANDOR

### *Rose Aylmer*

Ah, what avails the sceptred race!
   Ah, what the form divine!
What every virtue, every grace!
   Rose Aylmer, all were thine.

Rose Aylmer, whom these wakeful eyes
   May weep, but never see,
A night of memories and sighs
   I consecrate to thee.

FROM *The Vicar of Wakefield*

When lovely woman stoops to folly,
  And finds too late that men betray,
What charm can soothe her melancholy,
  What art can wash her guilt away?

The only art her guilt to cover,
  To hide her shame from every eye,
To give repentance to her lover,
  And wring his bosom, is – to die.

## DANTE GABRIEL ROSSETTI

### *Sudden Light*

I have been here before,
　　But when or how I cannot tell:
I know the grass beyond the door,
　　The sweet keen smell,
The sighing sound, the lights around the shore.

You have been mine before, –
　　How long ago I may not know:
But just when at that swallow's soar
　　Your neck turned so,
Some veil did fall, – I knew it all of yore.

Has this been thus before?
　　And shall not thus time's eddying flight
Still with our lives our love restore
　　In death's despite,
And day and night yield one delight once more?

*(Sonnet 40 from 'The House of Life:*
*A Sonnet Sequence')*

## *Severed Selves*

Two separate divided silences,
   Which, brought together, would find loving voice;
   Two glances which together would rejoice
In love, now lost like stars beyond dark trees;
Two hands apart whose touch alone gives ease;
   Two bosoms which, heart-shrined with mutual
                       flame,
   Would, meeting in one clasp, be made the same;
Two souls, the shore wave mocked of sundering
                    seas: –

Such are we now. Ah! may our hope forecast
   Indeed one hour again, when on this stream
   Of darkened love once more the light shall gleam? –
An hour how slow to come, how quickly past, –
Which blooms and fades, and only leaves at last,
   Faint as shed flowers, the attenuated dream.

### RALPH WALDO EMERSON

## *Celestial Love (Part of Ode I)*

Higher far,
Upward, into the pure realm,
Over sun or star,
Over the flickering Daemon film,
Thou must mount for love, –
Into vision which all form
In one only form dissolves;
In a region where the wheel,
On which all beings ride,
Visibly revolves;
Where the starred eternal worm
Girds the world with bound and term;
Where unlike things are like,
When good and ill,
And joy and moan,
Melt into one.
There Past, Present, Future, shoot
Triple blossoms from one root
Substances at base divided
In their summits are united,
There the holy Essence rolls,
One through separated souls,
And the sunny Aeon sleeps
Folding nature in its deeps,
And every fair and every good
Known in part or known impure
To men below,
In their archetypes endure.

The race of gods,

Or those we erring own,
Are shadows flitting up and down
In the still abodes.
The circles of that sea are laws,
Which publish and which hide the Cause.
Pray for a beam
Out of that sphere
Thee to guide and to redeem.
O what a load
Of care and toil
By lying Use bestowed,
From his shoulders falls, who sees
The true astronomy,
The period of peace!
Counsel which the ages kept,
Shall the well-born soul accept.
As the overhanging trees
Fill the lake with images,
As garment draws the garment's hem
Men their fortunes bring with them;
By right or wrong,
Lands and goods go to the strong;
Property will brutely draw
Still to the proprietor,
Silver to silver creep and wind,
And kind to kind,
Nor less the eternal poles
Of tendency distribute souls.
There need no vows to bind
Whom not each other seek but find.
They give and take no pledge or oath,
Nature is the bond of both.
No prayer persuades, no flattery fawns,
Their noble meanings are their pawns.
Plain and cold is their address,

Power have they for tenderness,
And so thoroughly is known
Each others' purpose by his own,
They can parley without meeting,
Need is none of forms of greeting,
They can well communicate
In their innermost estate;
When each the other shall avoid,
Shall each by each be most enjoyed.
Not with scarfs or perfumed gloves
Do these celebrate their loves,
Not by jewels, feasts, and savours,
Not by ribbons or by favours,
But by the sun-spark on the sea,
And the cloud-shadow on the lea,
The soothing lapse of morn to mirk,
And the cheerful round of work.
Their cords of love so public are,
They intertwine the farthest star.
The throbbing sea, the quaking earth,
Yield sympathy and signs of mirth;
Is none so high, so mean is none,
But feels and seals this union.
Even the tell Furies are appeased,
The good applaud, the lost are eased.

Love's hearts are faithful, but not fond,
Bound for the just, but not beyond;
Not glad, as the low-loving herd,
Of self in others still preferred,
But they have heartily designed
The benefit of broad mankind.
And they serve men austerely,
After their own genius, clearly,
Without a false humility;

For this is love's nobility,
Not to scatter bread and gold,
Goods and raiment bought and sold,
But to hold fast his simple sense,
And speak the speech of innocence,
And with hand, and body, and blood,
To make his bosom-counsel good:
For he that feeds men, serveth few,
He serves all, who dares be true.


RALPH WALDO EMERSON

*Eros*

The sense of the world is short,
Long and various the report,
To love and be beloved;
Men and gods have not outlearned it;
And, how oft soe'er they've turned it,
'Tis not to be improved.

## *Love – Thou art High*

Love – thou art high –
I cannot climb thee –
But, were it Two –
Who knows but we –
Taking turns – at the Chimborazo –
Ducal – at last – stand up by thee –

Love – thou art deep –
I cannot cross thee –
But, were there Two
Instead of One –
Rower, and Yacht – some sovereign Summer –
Who knows – but we'd reach the Sun?

Love – thou art Veiled –
A few – behold thee –
Smile – and alter – and prattle – and die –
Bliss – were an Oddity – without thee –
Nicknamed by God –
Eternity –

## EMILY DICKINSON

### *The Love a Life Can Show Below*

The Love a Life can show Below
Is but a filament, I know,
Of that diviner thing
That faints upon the face of Noon –
And smites the Tinder in the Sun –
And hinders Gabriel's Wing –

'Tis this – in Music – hints and sways –
And far abroad on Summer days –
Distils uncertain pain –
'Tis this enamours in the East –
And tints the Transit in the West
With harrowing Iodine –

'Tis this – invites – appalls – endows –
Flits – glimmers – proves – dissolves –
Returns – suggests – convicts – enchants –
Then – flings in Paradise –

## Love

Love – is that later Thing than Death –
More previous – than Life –
Confirms it at its entrance – And
Usurps it – of itself –

Tastes Death – the first – to hand the sting
The Second – to its friend –
Disarms the little interval –
Deposits Him with God –

Then hovers – an inferior Guard –
Lest this Beloved Charge
Need – once in an Eternity –
A smaller than the Large –


EMILY DICKINSON

## A Charm Invests a Face

A Charm invests a face
Imperfectly beheld –
The Lady dare not lift her Veil
For fear it be dispelled –

But peers beyond her mesh –
And wishes – and denies –
Lest Interview – annul a want
That Image – satisfies –

## EMILY DICKINSON

### Heart! We will Forget Him!

Heart! We will forget him!
You and I – tonight!
You may forget the warmth he gave –
I will forget the light!

When you have done, pray tell me
That I may straight begin!
Haste! lest while you're lagging
I remember him!

## EMILY DICKINSON

### Wild Nights

Wild nights – Wild nights!
Were I with thee
Wild nights should be
Our luxury!

Futile – the winds –
To a heart in port –
Done with the compass –
Done with the chart!

Rowing in Eden –
Ah – the sea!
Might I but moor –
Tonight – in thee!

EMILY DICKINSON

## *Come Slowly – Eden!*

Come slowly – Eden!
Lips unused to Thee –
Bashful – sip thy Jessamines –
As the fainting Bee –

Reaching late his flower,
Round her chamber hums –
Counts his nectars –
Enters – and is lost in Balms.

EMILY DICKINSON

## *He Fumbles at Your Spirit*

He fumbles at your spirit
As Players at the Keys
Before they drop full Music on –
He stuns you by degrees –
Prepares your brittle Nature
For the Ethereal Blow
By fainter Hammers – further heard –
Then nearer – Then so slow
Your Breath has time to straighten –
Your Brain – to bubble Cool –
Deals – One – imperial – Thunderbolt –
That scalps your naked Soul –

When Winds take Forests in the Paws –
The Universe – is still –

EMILY DICKINSON

## *I Gave Myself to Him*

I gave myself to Him –
And took Himself, for Pay,
The solemn contract of a Life
Was ratified, this way –

The Wealth might disappoint –
Myself a poorer prove
Than this great Purchaser suspect,
The Daily Own – of Love

Depreciate the Vision –
But till the Merchant buy –
Still Fable – in the Isles of Spice –
The subtle Cargoes – lie –

At least – 'tis Mutual – Risk –
Some – found it – Mutual Gain –
Sweet Debt of Life – Each Night to owe –
Insolvent – every Noon –

PHILIP BOURKE MARSTON

## *Inseparable*

When thou and I are dead, my dear,
  The earth above us lain;
When we no more in autumn hear
  The fall of leaves and rain,
Or round the snow-enshrouded year
  The midnight winds complain;

When we no more in green mid-spring,
  Its sights and sounds may mind, –
The warm wet leaves set quivering
  With touches of the wind,
The birds at morn, and birds that sing
  When day is left behind;

When, over all, the moonlight lies,
  Intensely bright and still;
When some meandering brooklet sighs
  At parting from its hill,
And scents from voiceless gardens rise,
  The peaceful air to fill;

When we no more through summer light
  The deep dim woods discern,
Nor hear the nightingales at night,
  In vehement singing, yearn
To stars and moon, that dumb and bright,
  In nightly vigil burn;

When smiles and hopes and joys and fears
  And words that lovers say,

And sighs of love, and passionate tears
    Are lost to us, for aye, –
What thing of all our love appears,
    In cold and coffined clay?

When all their kisses, sweet and close,
    Our lips shall quite forget;
When, where the day upon us rose,
    The day shall rise and set,
While we for love's sublime repose,
    Shall have not one regret, –

Oh, this true comfort is, I think,
    That, be death near or far,
When we have crossed the fatal brink,
    And found nor moon nor star,
We know not, when in death we sink,
    The lifeless things we are.

Yet one thought is, I deem, more kind,
    That when we sleep so well,
On memories that we leave behind
    When kindred souls shall dwell,
My name to thine in words they'll bind
    Of love inseparable.

EDWARD LEAR

## The Owl and the Pussy-cat

I

The Owl and the Pussy-cat went to sea
    In a beautiful pea-green boat,
They took some honey, and plenty of money,
    Wrapped up in a five-pound note.
The Owl looked up to the stars above,
    And sang to a small guitar,
'O lovely Pussy! O Pussy, my love,
    What a beautiful Pussy you are,
            You are,
            You are!
What a beautiful Pussy you are!'

2

Pussy said to the Owl, 'You elegant fowl!
    How charmingly sweet you sing!
O let us be married! too long we have tarried:
    But what shall we do for a ring?'
They sailed away, for a year and a day,
    To the land where the Bong-Tree grows
And there in a wood a Piggy-wig stood
    With a ring at the end of his nose,
            His nose,
            His nose,
    With a ring at the end of his nose.

3

'Dear Pig, are you willing to sell for one shilling
    Your ring?' Said the Piggy, 'I will.'

So they took it away, and were married next day
    By the Turkey who lives on the hill.
They dined on mince, and slices of quince,
    Which they ate with a runcible spoon;
And hand in hand, on the edge of the sand,
    They danced by the light of the moon,
        The moon,
        The moon,
They danced by the light of the moon.

*Love Poetry*

## *To Marguerite – Continued*

Yes! in the sea of life enisled,
   With echoing straits between us thrown,
Dotting the shoreless watery wild,
   We mortal millions live *alone*.
The islands feel the enclasping flow,
And then their endless bounds they know.

But when the moon their hollows lights,
   And they are swept by balms of spring,
And in their glens, on starry nights,
   The nightingales divinely sing;
And lovely notes, from shore to shore,
Across the sounds and channels pour –

O! then a longing like despair
   Is to their farthest caverns sent;
For surely once, they feel, we were
   Parts of a single continent!
Now round us spreads the watery plain –
O might our marges meet again!

Who ordered that their longing's fire
   Should be, as soon as kindled, cooled?
Who renders vain their deep desire? –
   A God, a God their severance ruled!
And bade betwixt their shores to be
The unplumbed, salt, estranging sea.

## ROBERT BROWNING

## *Life in a Love*

Escape me?
Never –
Beloved!
While I am I, and you are you,
   So long as the world contains us both,
   Me the loving and you the loth,
While the one eludes, must the other pursue.
My life is a fault at last, I fear:
   It seems too much like a fate, indeed!
   Though I do my best I shall scarce succeed.
But what if I fail of my purpose here?
It is but to keep the nerves at strain,
   To dry one's eyes and laugh at a fall,
And, baffled, get up and begin again, –
   So the chase takes up one's life, that's all.
While, look but once from your farthest bound
   At me so deep in the dust and dark,
No sooner the old hope goes to ground
   Than a new one, straight to the self-same mark,
I shape me –
Ever
Removed!

ROBERT BROWNING

## Love in a Life

Room after room,
I hunt the house through
We inhabit together.
Heart, fear nothing, for, heart, thou shalt find her –
Next time, herself! – not the trouble behind her
Left in the curtain, the couch's perfume!
As she brushed it, the cornice-wreath blossomed anew:
Yon looking-glass gleamed at the wave of her feather.

Yet the day wears,
And door succeeds door;
I try the fresh fortune –
Range the wide house from the wing to the centre.
Still the same chance! she goes out as I enter.
Spend my whole day in the quest, – who cares?
But 'tis twilight, you see, – with such suites to explore,
Such closets to search, such alcoves to importune!

## ROBERT BROWNING

### *Meeting at Night*

The grey sea and the long black land;
And the yellow half-moon large and low;
And the startled little waves that leap
In fiery ringlets from their sleep,
As I gain the cove with pushing prow,
And quench its speed i' the slushy sand.

Then a mile of warm sea-scented beach;
Three fields to cross till a farm appears;
A tap at the pane, the quick sharp scratch
And blue spurt of a lighted match,
And a voice less loud, thro' its joys and fears,
Than the two hearts beating each to each!

*Love Poetry*

## ROBERT BROWNING

### *My Last Duchess*

That's my last Duchess painted on the wall,
Looking as if she were alive. I call
That piece a wonder, now: Fra Pandolf's hands
Worked busily a day, and there she stands.
Will't please you sit and look at her? I said
'Fra Pandolf' by design, for never read
Strangers like you that pictured countenance,
The depth and passion of its earnest glance,
But to myself they turned (since none puts by
The curtain I have drawn for you, but I)
And seemed as they would ask me, if they durst,
How such a glance came there; so, not the first
Are you to turn and ask thus. Sir, 'twas not
Her husband's presence only, called that spot
Of joy into the Duchess' cheek; perhaps
Fra Pandolf chanced to say, 'Her mantle laps
Over my lady's wrist too much,' or 'Paint
Must never hope to reproduce the faint
Half-flush that dies along her throat.' Such stuff
Was courtesy, she thought, and cause enough
For calling up that spot of joy. She had
A heart – how shall I say? – too soon made glad,
Too easily impressed; she liked whate'er
She looked on, and her looks went everywhere.
Sir, 'twas all one! My favour at her breast,
The dropping of the daylight in the West,
The bough of cherries some officious fool
Broke in the orchard for her, the white mule
She rode with round the terrace – all and each
Would draw from her alike the approving speech,

Or blush, at least. She thanked men – good!
                               but thanked
Somehow – I know not how – as if she ranked
My gift of a nine-hundred-years-old name
With anybody's gift. Who'd stoop to blame
This sort of trifling? Even had you skill
In speech – which I have not – to make your will
Quite clear to such an one, and say, 'Just this
Or that in you disgusts me; here you miss,
Or there exceed the mark' – and if she let
Herself be lessoned so, nor plainly set
Her wits to yours, forsooth, and made excuse –
E'en then would be some stooping; and I choose
Never to stoop. Oh, sir, she smiled, no doubt,
Whene'er I passed her; but who passed without
Much the same smile? This grew; I gave commands;
Then all smiles stopped together. There she stands
As if alive. Will't please you rise? We'll meet
The company below, then. I repeat,
The Count your master's known munificence
Is ample warrant that no just pretence
Of mine for dowry will be disallowed;
Though his fair daughter's self, as I avowed
At starting, is my object. Nay, we'll go
Together down, sir. Notice Neptune, though,
Taming a sea-horse, thought a rarity,
Which Claus of Innsbruck cast in bronze for me!

## ROBERT BROWNING

### *Porphyria's Lover*

The rain set early in tonight,
    The sullen wind was soon awake,
It tore the elm-tops down for spite,
    And did its worst to vex the lake:
    I listened with heart fit to break.
When glided in Porphyria; straight
    She shut the cold out and the storm,
And kneeled and made the cheerless grate
    Blaze up, and all the cottage warm;
    Which done, she rose, and from her form
Withdrew the dripping cloak and shawl,
    And laid her soiled gloves by, untied
Her hat and let the damp hair fall,
    And, last, she sat down by my side
    And called me. When no voice replied,
She put my arm about her waist,
    And made her smooth white shoulder bare,
And all her yellow hair displaced,
    And, stooping, made my cheek lie there,
    And spread, o'er all, her yellow hair,
Murmuring how she loved me – she
    Too weak, for all her heart's endeavour,
To set its struggling passion free
    From pride, and vainer ties dissever,
    And give herself to me for ever.
But passion sometimes would prevail,
    Nor could tonight's gay feast restrain
A sudden thought of one so pale
    For love of her, and all in vain:
    So, she was come through wind and rain.

Be sure I looked up at her eyes
    Happy and proud; at last I knew
Porphyria worshipped me; surprise
    Made my heart swell, and still it grew
    While I debated what to do.
That moment she was mine, mine, fair,
    Perfectly pure and good: I found
A thing to do, and all her hair
    In one long yellow string I wound
    Three times her little throat around,
And strangled her. No pain felt she;
    I am quite sure she felt no pain.
As a shut bud that holds a bee,
    I warily oped her lids: again
    Laughed the blue eyes without a stain.
And I untightened next the tress
    About her neck; her cheek once more
Blushed bright beneath my burning kiss:
    I propped her head up as before,
    Only, this time my shoulder bore
Her head, which droops upon it still:
    The smiling rosy little head,
So glad it has its utmost will,
    That all it scorned at once is fled,
    And I, its love, am gained instead!
Porphyria's love: she guessed not how
    Her darling one wish would be heard.
And thus we sit together now,
    And all night long we have not stirred,
    And yet God has not said a word!

*Love Poetry*

## ROBERT BROWNING

### *You'll Love Me Yet and I Can Tarry*

You'll love me yet and I can tarry
Your love's protracted growing:
June reared that bunch of flowers you carry
From seeds of April's sowing.

I plant a heartful now: some seed
At least is sure to strike,
And yield what you'll not pluck indeed,
Not love, but, may be, like!

You'll look at least on love's remains,
A grave's one violet:
Your look? that pays a thousand pains.
What's death? You'll love me yet!

ROBERT BROWNING

## The Lost Mistress

All's over, then: does truth sound bitter
   As one at first believes?
Hark, 'tis the sparrows' good-night twitter
   About your cottage eaves!

And the leaf-buds on the vine are woolly,
   I noticed that, today;
One day more bursts them open fully
   – You know the red turns grey.

Tomorrow we meet the same then, dearest?
   May I take your hand in mine?
Mere friends are we, – well, friends the merest
   Keep much that I resign:

For each glance of the eye so bright and black,
   Though I keep with heart's endeavour, –
Your voice, when you wish the snowdrops back,
   Though it stay in my soul for ever! –

Yet I will but say what mere friends say,
   Or only a thought stronger;
I will hold your hand but as long as all may,
   Or so very little longer!

## FROM *'In a Gondola'*

The moth's kiss, first!
Kiss me as if you made believe
You were not sure, this eve,
How my face, your flower, had pursed
Its petals up; so, here and there
You brush it, till I grow aware
Who wants me, and wide ope I burst.

The bee's kiss, now!
Kiss me as if you entered gay
My heart at some noonday,
A bud that dares not disallow
The claim, so all is rendered up,
And passively its shattered cup
Over your head to sleep I bow.

**ROBERT BROWNING**

## *Eyes, Calm Beside Thee*

Eyes, calm beside thee (Lady, could'st thou know!)
    May turn away thick with fast-gathering tears:
I glance not where all gaze: thrilling and low
    Their passionate praises reach thee – my cheek wears
    Alone no wonder when thou passest by;
    Thy tremulous lids, bent and suffused, reply
To the irrepressible homage which doth glow
    On every lip but mine: if in thine ears
Their accents linger – and thou dost recall
    Me as I stood, still, guarded, very pale,
    Beside each votarist whose lighted brow
Wore worship like an aureole, 'O'er them all
    My beauty,' thou wilt murmur, 'did prevail
Save that one only:' – Lady, couldst thou know!

WALT WHITMAN

## Out of the Rolling Ocean

Out of the rolling ocean the crowd came a
                            drop gently to me,
Whispering, I love you, before long I die,
I have travell'd a long way merely to look on
                            you to touch you,
For I could not die till I once look'd on you,
For I fear'd I might afterward lose you.

Now we have met, we have look'd, we are safe,
Return in peace to the ocean my love,
I too am part of that ocean, my love, we are not
                            so much separated,
Behold the great rondure, the cohesion of all,
                            how perfect!
But as for me, for you, the irresistible sea is
                            to separate us,
As for an hour carrying us diverse, yet
                    cannot carry us diverse forever;
Be not impatient – a little space – know you
            I salute the air, the ocean and the land,
Every day at sundown for your dear sake,
                            my love.

WALT WHITMAN

## *As If a Phantom Caress'd Me*

As if a phantom caress'd me,
I thought I was not alone walking here by the shore;
But the one I thought was with me as now I walk
    by the shore, the one I loved that caress'd me,
As I lean and look through the glimmering light,
    that one has utterly disappear'd.
And those appear that are hateful to me and
    mock me.

WALT WHITMAN

## *Fast-Anchor'd Eternal O Love!*

Fast-anchor'd eternal O love! O woman I love!
O bride! O wife! more resistless than I can tell,
                    the thought of you!
Then separate, as disembodied or another born,
Ethereal, the last athletic reality, my consolation,
I ascend, I float in the regions of your love O man,
O sharer of my roving life.

**WALT WHITMAN**

## To a Stranger

Passing stranger! you do not know
How longingly I look upon you,
You must be he I was seeking,
Or she I was seeking
(It comes to me as a dream)
I have somewhere surely
Lived a life of joy with you,
All is recall'd as we flit by each other,
Fluid, affectionate, chaste, matured,
You grew up with me,
Were a boy with me or a girl with me,
I ate with you and slept with you, your body has
    become not yours only nor left my body mine
    only,
You give me the pleasure of your eyes, face, flesh as
    we pass,
You take of my beard, breast, hands, in return,
I am not to speak to you, I am to think of you when
    I sit alone or wake at night, alone
I am to wait, I do not doubt I am to meet you again
I am to see to it that I do not lose you.

# WALT WHITMAN

## *When I Heard at the Close of the Day*

When I heard at the close of the day how my name
    had been receiv'd with plaudits in the capitol,
    still it was not a happy night for me that
    follow'd,
And else when I carous'd, or when my plans were
    accomplish'd, still I was not happy,
But the day when I rose at dawn from the bed of
    perfect health, refresh'd, singing, inhaling the
    ripe breath of autumn,
When I saw the full moon in the west grow pale and
    disappear in the morning light,
When I wander'd alone over the beach, and
    undressing bathed, laughing with the cool
    waters, and saw the sun rise,
And when I thought how my dear friend my lover
    was on his way coming, O then I was happy,
O then each breath tasted sweeter, and all that day
    my food nourish'd me more, and the beautiful
    day pass'd well,
And the next came with equal joy, and with the
    next at evening came my friend,
And that night while all was still I heard the waters
    roll slowly continually up the shores,
I heard the hissing rustle of the liquid and sands as
    directed to me whispering to congratulate me,
For the one I love most lay sleeping by me under
    the same cover in the cool night,
In the stillness in the autumn moonbeams his face
    was inclined toward me,
And his arm lay lightly around my breast – and that
    night I was happy.

*Love Poetry*

## ALFRED, LORD TENNYSON

### FROM 'The Princess'

Tears, idle tears, I know not what they mean,
Tears from the depth of some divine despair
Rise in the heart, and gather to the eyes,
In looking on the happy Autumn-fields,
And thinking of the days that are no more.

Fresh as the first beam glittering on a sail,
That brings our friends up from the underworld,
Sad as the last which reddens over one
That sinks with all we love below the verge;
So sad, so fresh, the days that are no more.

Ah, sad and strange as in dark summer dawns
The earliest pipe of half-awaken'd birds
To dying ears, when unto dying eyes
The casement slowly grows a glimmering square;
So sad, so strange, the days that are no more.

Dear as remember'd kisses after death,
And sweet as those by hopeless fancy feign'd
On lips that are for others; deep as love,
Deep as first love, and wild with all regret;
O Death in Life, the days that are no more!

ALFRED LORD TENNYSON

FROM *'The Princess'*

Now sleeps the crimson petal, now the white;
Nor waves the cypress in the palace walk;
Nor winks the gold fin in the porphyry font;
The firefly wakens, waken thou with me.

Now droops the milk-white peacock like a ghost,
And like a ghost she glimmers on to me.

Now lies the Earth all Danaë to the stars,
And all thy heart lies open unto me.

Now slides the silent meteor on, and leaves
A shining furrow, as thy thoughts, in me.

Now folds the lily all her sweetness up,
And slips into the bosom of the lake.
So fold thyself, my dearest, thou, and slip
Into my bosom and be lost in me.

*Love Poetry*

ALFRED, LORD TENNYSON

## Marriage Morning

Light, so low upon earth,
    You send a flash to the sun.
Here is the golden close of love,
    All my wooing is done.
Oh, all the woods and the meadows,
    Woods, where we hid from the wet,
Stiles where we stayed to be kind,
    Meadows in which we met!

Light, so low in the vale
    You flash and lighten afar,
For this is the golden morning of love,
    And you are his morning star.
Flash, I am coming, I come,
    By meadow and stile and wood,
Oh, lighten into my eyes and my heart,
    Into my heart and my blood!

Heart, are you great enough
    For a love that never tires?
O heart, are you great enough for love?
    I have heard of thorns and briers.
Over the thorns and briers,
    Over the meadows and stiles,
Over the world to the end of it
    Flash of a million miles.

ALFRED, LORD TENNYSON

# In the Valley of Cauteretz

All along the valley, stream that flashest white,
Deepening thy voice with the deepening of the night,
All along the valley, where thy waters flow,
I walked with one I loved two and thirty years ago.
All along the valley, while I walked today,
The two and thirty years were a mist that rolls away;
For all along the valley, down thy rocky bed,
Thy living voice to me was as the voice of the dead,
And all along the valley, by rock and cave and tree,
The voice of the dead was a living voice to me.


ALFRED, LORD TENNYSON

# If I were Loved

If I were loved, as I desire to be,
What is there in this great sphere of earth,
And range of evil between death and birth,
That I should fear, – if I were loved by thee?
All the inner, all the outer world of pain
Clear Love would pierce and cleave, if thou wert mine,
As I have heard that, somewhere in the main,
Fresh-water springs come up through bitter brine.
'Twere joy, not fear, claspt hand-in-hand with thee,
To wait for death – mute – careless of all ills,
Apart upon a mountain, through the surge
Of some new deluge from a thousand hills
Flung leagues of roaring foam into the gorge
Below us, as far on as eye could see.

*Love Poetry*

## ALFRED, LORD TENNYSON

### FROM *Maud*

Come into the garden, Maud,
　For the black bat, night, has flown,
Come into the garden, Maud,
　I am here at the gate alone;
And the woodbine spices are wafted abroad,
　And the musk of the rose is blown.

For a breeze of morning moves,
　And the planet of Love is on high,
Beginning to faint in the light that she loves
　In a bed of daffodil sky,
To faint in the light of the sun she loves,
　To faint in his light, and to die.

## ALFRED, LORD TENNYSON

### FROM *In Memoriam A. H. H.*

I envy not in any moods
    The captive void of noble rage,
    The linnet born within the cage,
That never knew the summer woods:

I envy not the beast that takes
    His license in the field of time,
    Unfetter'd by the sense of crime,
To whom a conscience never wakes;

Nor, what may count itself as blest,
    The heart that never plighted troth
    But stagnates in the weeds of sloth;
Nor any want-begotten rest.

I hold it true, whate'er befall;
    I feel it, when I sorrow most;
    'Tis better to have loved and lost
Than never to have loved at all.

*Love Poetry*

CHRISTINA ROSSETTI

## *The First Day*

I wish I could remember that first day,
  First hour, first moment of your meeting me,
  If bright or dim the season, it might be
Summer or Winter for aught I can say;
So unrecorded did it slip away,
  So blind was I to see and to foresee,
  So dull to mark the budding of my tree
That would not blossom yet for many a May.
If only I could recollect it, such
  A day of days! I let it come and go
  As traceless as a thaw of bygone snow;
It seemed to mean so little, meant so much;
If only now I could recall that touch,
  First touch of hand in hand – Did one but know!

## CHRISTINA ROSSETTI

### *Somewhere or Other*

Somewhere or other there must surely be
   The face not seen, the voice not heard,
The heart that not yet – never yet – ah me!
   Made answer to my word.

Somewhere or other, may be near or far;
   Past land and sea, clean out of sight;
Beyond the wandering moon, beyond the star
   That tracks her night by night.

Somewhere or other, may be far or near;
   With just a wall, a hedge, between;
With just the last leaves of the dying year
   Fallen on a turf grown green.

CHRISTINA ROSSETTI

## A Birthday

My heart is like a singing bird
   Whose nest is in a watered shoot;
My heart is like an apple-tree
   Whose boughs are bent with thickset fruit;
My heart is like a rainbow shell
   That paddles in a halcyon sea;
My heart is gladder than all these
   Because my love is come to me.

Raise me a dais of silk and down;
   Hang it with vair and purple dyes;
Carve it in doves and pomegranates,
   And peacocks with a hundred eyes;
Work it in gold and silver grapes,
   In leaves and silver fleurs-de-lys;
Because the birthday of my life
   Is come, my love is come to me.


CHRISTINA ROSSETTI

## A Bride Song

Too late for love, too late for joy,
   Too late, too late!
You loitered on the road too long,
   You trifled at the gate:
The enchanted dove upon her branch
   Died without a mate;

The enchanted princess in her tower
  Slept, died, behind the grate;
Her heart was starving all this while
  You made it wait.

Ten years ago, five years ago,
  One year ago,
Even then you had arrived in time,
  Though somewhat slow;
Then you had known her living face
  Which now you cannot know:
The frozen fountain would have leaped,
  The buds gone on to blow,
The warm south wind would have awaked
  To melt the snow.

Is she fair now as she lies?
  Once she was fair;
Meet queen for any kingly king,
  With gold-dust on her hair,
Now these are poppies in her locks,
  White poppies she must wear;
Must wear a veil to shroud her face
  And the want graven there:
Or is the hunger fed at length,
  Cast off the care?

We never saw her with a smile
  Or with a frown;
Her bed seemed never soft to her,
  Though tossed of down;
She little heeded what she wore,
  Kirtle, or wreath, or gown;
We think her white brows often ached
  Beneath her crown,

Till silvery hairs showed in her locks
    That used to be so brown.

We never heard her speak in haste;
    Her tones were sweet,
And modulated just so much
    As it was meet:
Her heart sat silent through the noise
    And concourse of the street.
There was no hurry in her hands,
    No hurry in her feet;
There was no bliss drew nigh to her,
    That she might run to greet.

You should have wept her yesterday,
    Wasting upon her bed:
But wherefore should you weep today
    That she is dead?
Lo we who love weep not today,
    But crown her royal head.
Let be these poppies that we strew,
    Your roses are too red:
Let be these poppies, not for you
    Cut down and spread.

## *Mirage*

The hope I dreamed of was a dream,
    Was but a dream; and now I wake,
Exceeding comfortless, and worn, and old,
    For a dream's sake.

I hang my harp upon a tree,
    A weeping willow in a lake;
I hang my silenced harp there, wrung and snapt
    For a dream's sake.

Lie still, lie still, my breaking heart;
    My silent heart, lie still and break:
Life, and the world, and mine own self, are changed
    For a dream's sake.

CHRISTINA ROSSETTI

## I Loved You First

Poca favilla gran fiamma seconda.

DANTE

Ogni altra cosa, ogni pensier va fore,
E sol ivi con voi rimansi amore.

PETRARCA

I loved you first: but afterwards your love
   Outsoaring mine, sang such a loftier song
As drowned the friendly cooings of my dove.
   Which owes the other most? my love was long,
   And yours one moment seemed to wax more strong;
I loved and guessed at you, you construed me
   And loved me for what might or might not be –
   Nay, weights and measures do us both a wrong.
For verily love knows not 'mine' or 'thine';
   With separate 'I' and 'thou' free love has done,
   For one is both and both are one in love:
Rich love knows nought of 'thine that is not mine';
   Both have the strength and both the length thereof,
Both of us, of the love which makes us one.

## CHRISTINA ROSSETTI

### *Echo*

Come to me in the silence of the night;
　　Come in the speaking silence of a dream;
Come with soft rounded cheeks and eyes as bright
　　As sunlight on a stream;
　　　Come back in tears,
O memory, hope, love of finished years.

O dream how sweet, too sweet, too bitter-sweet,
　　Whose wakening should have been in Paradise,
Where souls brimfull of love abide and meet;
　　Where thirsting longing eyes
　　　Watch the slow door
That opening, letting in, lets out no more.

Yet come to me in dreams, that I may live
　　My very life again though cold in death;
Come back to me in dreams, that I may give
　　Pulse for pulse, breath for breath:
　　　Speak low, lean low,
As long ago, my love, how long ago.

## *Many in Aftertimes will Say of You*

Vien dietro a me e lascia dir le genti.

DANTE

Contando i casi della vita nostra.

PETRARCA

Many in aftertimes will say of you
  'He loved her' – while of me what will they say?
  Not that I loved you more than just in play,
For fashion's sake as idle women do.
Even let them prate; who know not what we knew
  Of love and parting in exceeding pain.
  Of parting hopeless here to meet again,
Hopeless on earth, and heaven is out of view.
But by my heart of love laid bare to you.
  My love that you can make not void nor vain,
Love that foregoes you but to claim anew
  Beyond this passage of the gate of death,
I charge you at the Judgment make it plain
  My love of you was life and not a breath.

## CHRISTINA ROSSETTI

### *Remember*

Remember me when I am gone away,
    Gone far away into the silent land;
      When you can no more hold me by the hand,
Nor I half turn to go yet turning stay.
Remember me when no more day by day
    You tell me of our future that you plann'd:
      Only remember me; you understand
It will be late to counsel then or pray.
Yet if you should forget me for a while
    And afterwards remember, do not grieve:
    For if the darkness and corruption leave
      A vestige of the thoughts that once I had,
Better by far you should forget and smile
    Than that you should remember and be sad.

## CHRISTINA ROSSETTI

### *When I am Dead, my Dearest*

When I am dead, my dearest,
   Sing no sad songs for me;
Plant thou no roses at my head,
   Nor shady cypress tree:
Be the green grass above me
   With showers and dewdrops wet;
And if thou wilt, remember,
   And if thou wilt, forget.

I shall not see the shadows,
   I shall not feel the rain;
I shall not hear the nightingale
   Sing on, as if in pain:
And dreaming through the twilight
   That doth not rise nor set,
Haply I may remember,
   And haply may forget.

## The Kiss

'I saw you take his kiss!' ' 'Tis true.'
  'O, modesty!' ' 'Twas strictly kept:
He thought me asleep; at least I knew
  He thought I thought he thought I slept.'

## A Farewell

With all my will, but much against my heart,
We two now part.
My Very Dear,
Our solace is, the sad road lies so clear.
It needs no art,
With faint, averted feet
And many a tear,
In our opposed paths to persevere.
Go thou to East, I West.
We will not say
There's any hope, it is so far away.
But, O, my Best!
When the one darling of our widowhead,
The nursling Grief,
Is dead,
And no dews blur our eyes
To see the peach-bloom come in evening skies,
Perchance we may,
Where now this night is day,
And even through faith of still averted feet,
Making full circle of our banishment,
Amazed meet;
The bitter journey to the bourne so sweet
Seasoning the termless feast of our content
With tears of recognition never dry.

**ERNEST DOWSON**

*Non sum qualis eram bonae sub regno Cynarae*

Last night, ah, yesternight, betwixt her lips and mine
There fell thy shadow, Cynara! thy breath was shed
Upon my soul between the kisses and the wine;
And I was desolate and sick of an old passion,
   Yea, I was desolate and bowed my head:
I have been faithful to thee, Cynara! in my fashion.

All night upon mine heart I felt her warm heart beat,
Nightlong within mine arms in love and sleep she lay;
Surely the kisses of her bought red mouth were sweet;
But I was desolate and sick of an old passion,
   When I awoke and found the dawn was grey:
I have been faithful to thee, Cynara! in my fashion.

I have forgot much, Cynara! gone with the wind,
Flung roses, roses riotously with the throng,
Dancing, to put thy pale, lost lilies out of mind,
But I was desolate and sick of an old passion,
   Yea, all the time, because the dance was long:
I have been faithful to thee, Cynara! in my fashion.

I cried for madder music and for stronger wine,
But when the feast is finished and the lamps expire,
Then falls thy shadow, Cynara! the night is thine;
And I am desolate and sick of an old passion,
   Yea, hungry for the lips of my desire:
I have been faithful to thee, Cynara! in my fashion.

*Love Poetry*

ERNEST DOWSON

## Exile

By the sad waters of separation
   Where we have wandered by divers ways,
I have but the shadow and imitation
   Of the old memorial days.

In music I have no consolation,
   No roses are pale enough for me;
The sound of the waters of separation
   Surpasseth roses and melody.

By the sad waters of separation
   Dimly I hear from an hidden place
The sigh of mine ancient adoration:
   Hardly can I remember your face.

If you be dead, no proclamation
   Sprang to me over the waste, gray sea:
Living, the waters of separation
   Sever for ever your soul from me.

No man knoweth our desolation;
   Memory pales of the old delight;
While the sad waters of separation
   Bear us on to the ultimate night.

OSCAR WILDE

## *Helas!*

To drift with every passion till my soul
Is a stringed lute on which all winds can play,
Is it for this that I have given away
Mine ancient wisdom, and austere control?
Methinks my life is a twice-written scroll
Scrawled over on some boyish holiday
With idle songs for pipe and virelay,
Which do but mar the secret of the whole.
Surely there was a time I might have trod
The sunlit heights, and from life's dissonance
Struck one clear chord to reach the ears of God:
Is that time dead? lo! with a little rod
I did but touch the honey of romance –
And must I lose a soul's inheritance?

## Her Voice

The wild bee reels from bough to bough
With his furry coat and his gauzy wing.
Now in a lily-cup, and now
Setting a jacinth bell a-swing,
In his wandering;
Sit closer love: it was here I trow
I made that vow,

Swore that two lives should be like one
As long as the sea-gull loved the sea,
As long as the sunflower sought the sun, –
It shall be, I said, for eternity
'Twixt you and me!
Dear friend, those times are over and done,
Love's web is spun.

Look upward where the poplar trees
Sway and sway in the summer air,
Here in the valley never a breeze
Scatters the thistledown, but there
Great winds blow fair
From the mighty murmuring mystical seas,
And the wave-lashed leas.

Look upward where the white gull screams,
What does it see that we do not see?
Is that a star? or the lamp that gleams
On some outward voyaging argosy, –
Ah! can it be
We have lived our lives in a land of dreams!
How sad it seems.

Sweet, there is nothing left to say
But this, that love is never lost,
Keen winter stabs the breasts of May
Whose crimson roses burst his frost,
Ships tempest-tossed
Will find a harbour in some bay,
And so we may.

And there is nothing left to do
But to kiss once again, and part,
Nay, there is nothing we should rue,
I have my beauty – you your Art,
Nay, do not start,
One world was not enough for two
Like me and you.

OSCAR WILDE

## To My Wife

### With a Copy of My Poems

I can write no stately proem
As a prelude to my lay;
From a poet to a poem
I would dare to say.

For if of these fallen petals
One to you seem fair,
Love will waft it till it settles
On your hair.

And when wind and winter harden
All the loveless land,
It will whisper of the garden,
You will understand.

## SIR EDWIN ARNOLD

### *Destiny*

Somewhere there waiteth in this world of ours
For one lone soul another lonely soul
Each choosing each through all the weary hours
And meeting strangely at one sudden goal.
Then blend they, like green leaves with golden flowers,
Into one beautiful and perfect whole;
And life's long night is ended, and the way
Lies open onward to eternal day.

PAUL LAURENCE DUNBAR

## Invitation to Love

Come when the nights are bright with stars
Or come when the moon is mellow;
Come when the sun his golden bars
Drops on the hayfield yellow.
Come in the twilight soft and gray,
Come in the night or come in the day,
Come, O love, whene'er you may,
And you are welcome, welcome.

You are sweet, O Love, dear Love,
You are soft as the nesting dove.
Come to my heart and bring it to rest
As the bird flies home to its welcome nest.

Come when my heart is full of grief
Or when my heart is merry;
Come with the falling of the leaf
Or with the redd'ning cherry.
Come when the year's first blossom blows,
Come when the summer gleams and glows,
Come with the winter's drifting snows,
And you are welcome, welcome.

MARY COLERIDGE

## *My True Love Hath My Heart and I Have His*

None ever was in love with me but grief.
　She wooed me from the day that I was born;
She stole my playthings first, the jealous thief,
　And left me there forlorn.

The birds that in my garden would have sung,
　She scared away with her unending moan;
She slew my lovers too when I was young,
　And left me there alone.

Grief, I have cursed thee often – now at last
　To hate thy name I am no longer free;
Caught in thy bony arms and prisoned fast,
　I love no love but thee.

　　　　　　　　　　　　　　　　*Love Poetry*

## A. C. SWINBURNE

### *In the Orchard*

Leave go my hands, let me catch breath and see;
Let the dew-fall drench either side of me;
   Clear apple-leaves are soft upon that moon
Seen sidelong like a blossom in the tree;
    And God, ah God, that day should be so soon.

The grass is thick and cool, it lets us lie.
Kissed upon either cheek and either eye,
   I turn to thee as some green afternoon
Turns toward sunset, and is loth to die;
    Ah God, ah God, that day should be so soon.

Lie closer, lean your face upon my side,
Feel where the dew fell that has hardly dried,
   Hear how the blood beats that went nigh to swoon;
The pleasure lives there when the sense has died,
    Ah God, ah God, that day should be so soon.

O my fair lord, I charge you leave me this:
It is not sweeter than a foolish kiss?
   Nay take it then, my flower, my first in June,
My rose, so like a tender mouth it is:
    Ah God, ah God, that day should be so soon.

Love, till dawn sunder night from day with fire
Dividing my delight and my desire,
   The crescent life and love the plenilune,
Love me though dusk begin and dark retire;
    Ah God, ah God, that day should be so soon.

Ah, my heart fails, my blood draws back; I know,
When life runs over, life is near to go;
    And with the slain of love love's ways are strewn,
And with their blood, if love will have it so;
    Ah God, ah God, that day should be so soon.

Ah, do thy will now; slay me if thou wilt;
There is no building now the walls are built,
    No quarrying now the cornerstone is hewn,
No drinking now the vine's whole blood is spilt;
    Ah God, ah God, that day should be so soon.

Nay, slay me now; nay, for I will be slain;
Pluck thy red pleasure from the teeth of pain,
    Break down thy vine ere yet grape-gatherers prune,
Slay me ere day can slay desire again;
    Ah God, ah God, that day should be so soon.

Yea, with thy sweet lips, with thy sweet sword; yea
Take life and all, for I will die, I say;
    Love, I gave love, is life a better boon?
For sweet night's sake I will not live till day;
    Ah God, ah God, that day should be so soon.

Nay, I will sleep then only; nay, but go.
Ah sweet, too sweet to me, my sweet, I know
    Love, sleep, and death go to the sweet same tune;
Hold my hair fast, and kiss me through it soon.
    Ah God, ah God, that day should be so soon.

## *Love and Sleep*

Lying asleep between the strokes of night
   I saw my love lean over my sad bed,
   Pale as the duskiest lily's leaf or head,
Smooth-skinned and dark, with bare throat
                         made to bite,
Too wan for blushing and too warm for white,
   But perfect-coloured without white or red.
   And her lips opened amorously, and said –
I wist not what, saving one word – Delight.

And all her face was honey to my mouth,
   And all her body pasture to mine eyes;
     The long lithe arms and hotter hands
                         than fire,
The quivering flanks, hair smelling of the south,
   The bright light feet, the splendid supple thighs
     And glittering eyelids of my soul's desire.

## GEORGE MEREDITH

### FROM *Modern Love*

By this he knew she wept with waking eyes:
That, at his hand's light quiver by her head,
The strange low sobs that shook their common bed
Were called into her with a sharp surprise,
And strangled mute, like little gaping snakes,
Dreadfully venomous to him. She lay
Stone-still, and the long darkness flowed away
With muffled pulses. Then, as midnight makes
Her giant heart of Memory and Tears
Drink the pale drug of silence, and so beat
Sleep's heavy measure, they from head to feet
Were moveless, looking through their dead black years,
By vain regret scrawled over the blank wall.
Like sculptured effigies they might be seen
Upon their marriage-tomb, the sword between;
Each wishing for the sword that severs all.

## The Great Lover

I have been so great a lover: filled my days
So proudly with the splendour of Love's praise,
The pain, the calm, and the astonishment,
Desire illimitable, and still content,
And all dear names men use, to cheat despair,
For the perplexed and viewless streams that bear
Our hearts at random down the dark of life.
Now, ere the unthinking silence on that strife
Steals down, I would cheat drowsy Death so far,
My night shall be remembered for a star
That outshone all the suns of all men's days.
Shall I not crown them with immortal praise
Whom I have loved, who have given me, dared with me
High secrets, and in darkness knelt to see
The inenarrable godhead of delight?
Love is a flame – we have beaconed the world's night.
A city – and we have built it, these and I.
An emperor – we have taught the world to die.
So, for their sakes I loved, ere I go hence,
And the high cause of Love's magnificence,
And to keep loyalties young, I'll write those names
Golden for ever, eagles, crying flames,
And set them as a banner, that men may know,
To dare the generations, burn, and blow
Out on the wind of Time, shining and streaming . . .

These I have loved:
        White plates and cups, clean-gleaming,
Ringed with blue lines; and feathery, faery dust;
Wet roofs, beneath the lamp-light; the strong crust

Of friendly bread; and many-tasting food;
Rainbows; and the blue bitter smoke of wood;
And radiant raindrops couching in cool flowers;
And flowers themselves, that sway through sunny hours,
Dreaming of moths that drink them under the moon;
Then, the cool kindliness of sheets, that soon
Smooth away trouble; and the rough male kiss
Of blankets; grainy wood; live hair that is
Shining and free; blue-massing clouds; the keen
Unpassioned beauty of a great machine;
The benison of hot water; furs to touch;
The good smell of old clothes; and other such –
The comfortable smell of friendly fingers,
Hair's fragrance, and the musty reek that lingers
About dead leaves and last year's ferns . . .

                                        Dear names,
And thousand others throng to me! Royal flames;
Sweet water's dimpling laugh from tap or spring;
Holes in the ground; and voices that do sing;
Voices in laughter, too; and body's pain,
Soon turned to peace; and the deep-panting train;
Firm sands; the little dulling edge of foam
That browns and dwindles as the wave goes home;
And washen stones, gay for an hour; the cold
Graveness of iron; moist black earthen mould;
Sleep; and high places; footprints in the dew;
And oaks; and brown horse-chestnuts, glossy-new;
And new-peeled sticks; and shining pools on grass; –
All these have been my loves. And these shall pass,
Whatever passes not, in the great hour,
Nor all my passion, all my prayers, have power
To hold them with me through the gate of Death.
They'll play deserter, turn with the traitor breath,
Break the high bond we made, and sell Love's trust
And sacramented covenant to the dust.

– Oh, never a doubt but, somewhere, I shall wake,
And give what's left of love again, and make
New friends, now strangers . . .

                    But the best I've known
Stays here, and changes, breaks, grows old, is blown
About the winds of the world, and fades from brains
Of living men, and dies.

                    Nothing remains.

O dear my loves, O faithless, once again
This one last gift I give: that after men
Shall know, and later lovers, far-removed,
Praise you, 'All these were lovely'; say, 'He loved.'

## The Hill

Breathless, we flung us on the windy hill,
 Laughed in the sun, and kissed the lovely grass.
 You said, 'Though glory and ecstasy we pass;
Wind, sun and earth remain, the birds sing still,
When we are old, are old . . . ' And when we die
All's over that is ours; and life burns on
Through other lovers, other lips,' said I,
'Heart of my heart, our heaven is now, is won.'

'We are Earth's best, that learnt her lesson here.
 Life is our cry. We have kept the faith!' we said;
 'We shall go down with unreluctant tread
Rose-crowned into the darkness!' . . . Proud we were,
And laughed, that had such brave true things to say.
– And then you suddenly cried, and turned away.

## RUPERT BROOKE

### Sonnet

Oh! Death will find me, long before I tire
    Of watching you; and swing me suddenly
Into the shade and loneliness and mire
    Of the last land! There, waiting patiently,

One day, I think, I'll feel a cool wind blowing,
    See a slow light across the Stygian tide,
And hear the Dead about me stir, unknowing,
    And tremble. And *I* shall know that you have died,

And watch you, a broad-browed and smiling dream,
    Pass, light as ever, through the lightless host,
Quietly ponder, start, and sway, and gleam –
    Most individual and bewildering ghost! –

And turn, and toss your brown delightful head
Amusedly, among the ancient Dead.


## RUPERT BROOKE

### Retrospect

In your arms was still delight,
Quiet as a street at night;
And thoughts of you, I do remember,
Were green leaves in a darkened chamber,
Were dark clouds in a moonless sky.
Love, in you, went passing by,
Penetrative, remote, and rare,
Like a bird in the wide air,

And, as the bird, it left no trace
In the heaven of your face.
In your stupidity I found
The sweet hush after a sweet sound.
All about you was the light
That dims the greying end of night;
Desire was the unrisen sun,
Joy the day not yet begun,
With tree whispering to tree,
Without wind, quietly.
Wisdom slept within your hair,
And Long-Suffering was there,
And, in the flowing of your dress,
Undiscerning Tenderness.
And when you thought, it seemed to me,
Infinitely, and like a sea,
About the slight world you had known
Your vast unconsciousness was thrown . . .

O haven without wave or tide!
Silence, in which all songs have died!
Holy book, where all hearts are still!
And home at length, under the hill!
O mother quiet, breasts of peace,
Where love itself would faint and cease!
O infinite deep I never knew,
I would come back, come back to you,
Find you, as a pool unstirred,
Kneel down by you, and never a word,
Lay my head, and nothing said,
In your hands, ungarlanded;
And a long watch you would keep;
And I should sleep, and I should sleep!

*Love Poetry*

EDWARD THOMAS

## *No One So Much As You*

No one so much as you
Loves this my clay,
Or would lament as you
Its dying day.

You know me through and through
Though I have not told,
And though with what you know
You are not bold.

None ever was so fair
As I thought you:
Not a word can I bear
Spoken against you.

All that I ever did
For you seemed coarse
Compared with what I hid
Nor put in force.

My eyes scarce dare meet you
Lest they should prove
I but respond to you
And do not love.

We look and understand,
We cannot speak
Except in trifles and
Words the most weak.

For I at most accept
Your love, regretting
That is all: I have kept
Only a fretting

That I could not return
All that you gave
And could not ever burn
With the love you have,

Till sometimes it did seem
Better it were
Never to see you more
Than linger here

With only gratitude
Instead of love –
A pine in solitude
Cradling a dove.


EDWARD THOMAS

*Like the Touch of Rain*

Like the touch of rain she was
On a man's flesh and hair and eyes
When the joy of walking thus
Has taken him by surprise:

With the love of the storm he burns,
He sings, he laughs, well I know how,
But forgets when he returns
As I shall not forget her 'Go now'.

Those two words shut a door
Between me and the blessed rain
That was never shut before
And will not open again.

## *Greater Love*

Red lips are not so red
  As the stained stones kissed by the English dead.
Kindness of wooed and wooer
Seems shame to their love pure.
O Love, your eyes lose lure
  When I behold eyes blinded in my stead!

Your slender attitude
  Trembles not exquisite like limbs knife-skewed,
Rolling and rolling there
Where God seems not to care;
Till the fierce love they bear
  Cramps them in death's extreme decrepitude.

Your voice sings not so soft, –
  Though even as wind murmuring through
                                raftered loft, –
Your dear voice is not dear,
Gentle, and evening clear,
As theirs whom none now hear,
  Now earth has stopped their piteous mouths
                                that coughed.

Heart, you were never hot
  Nor large, nor full like hearts made great with shot;
And though your hand be pale,
Paler are all which trail
Your cross through flame and hail:
  Weep, you may weep, for you may touch them not.

## ALICE MEYNELL

### *Renouncement*

I must not think of thee; and, tired yet strong,
I shun the love that lurks in all delight –
   The thought of thee – and in the blue
                    heaven's height,
And in the sweetest passage of a song.
Oh, just beyond the fairest thoughts that throng
   This breast, the thought of thee waits hidden
                    yet bright;
But it must never, never come in sight;
I must stop short of thee the whole day long.
But when sleep comes to close each difficult day,
   When night gives pause to the long watch I keep,
And all my bonds I needs must loose apart,
Must doff my will as raiment laid away, –
   With the first dream that comes with the first sleep
I run, I run, I am gathered to thy heart.

THOMAS HARDY

## The Voice

Woman much missed, how you call to me, call to me,
Saying that now you are not as you were
When you had changed from the one who was all to me,
But as at first, when our day was fair.

Can it be you that I hear? Let me view you, then,
Standing as when I drew near to the town
Where you would wait for me: yes, as I knew you then,
Even to the original air-blue gown!

Or is it only the breeze, in its listlessness
Travelling across the wet mead to me here,
You being ever dissolved to wan wistlessness,
Heard no more again far or near?

    Thus I; faltering forward,
    Leaves around me falling,
Wind oozing thin through the thorn from norward,
    And the woman calling.

THOMAS HARDY

*The Going*

Why did you give no hint that night
That quickly after the morrow's dawn,
And calmly, as if indifferent quite,
You would close your term here, up and be gone
    Where I could not follow
    With wing of swallow
To gain one glimpse of you ever anon!

    Never to bid goodbye
    Or lip me the softest call,
Or utter a wish for a word, while I
Saw morning harden upon the wall,
    Unmoved, unknowing
    That your great going
Had place that moment, and altered all.

Why do you make me leave the house
And think for a breath it is you I see
At the end of the alley of bending boughs
Where so often at dusk you used to be;
    Till in darkening dankness
    The yawning blankness
Of the perspective sickens me!

    You were she who abode
    By those red-veined rocks far West,
You were the swan-necked one who rode
Along the beetling Beeny Crest,
    And, reining nigh me,
    Would muse and eye me,
While Life unrolled us its very best.

*Love Poetry*

Why, then, latterly did we not speak,
Did we not think of those days long dead,
And ere your vanishing strive to seek
That time's renewal? We might have said,
    'In this bright spring weather
    We'll visit together
Those places that once we visited.'

    Well, well! All's past amend,
    Unchangeable. It must go.
I seem but a dead man held on end
To sink down soon . . . O you could not know
    That such swift fleeing
    No soul foreseeing –
Not even I – would undo me so!

THOMAS HARDY

## After a Journey

Hereto I come to view a voiceless ghost;
　　Whither, O whither will its whim now draw me?
Up the cliff, down, till I'm lonely, lost,
　　And the unseen waters' ejaculations awe me.
Where you will next be there's no knowing,
　　Facing round about me everywhere,
　　　　With your nut-coloured hair,
And grey eyes, and rose-flush coming and going.

Yes: I have re-entered your olden haunts at last;
　　Through the years, through the dead scenes I
　　　　　　　　have tracked you;
What have you now found to say of our past –
　　Scanned across the dark space wherein I
　　　　　　　　　　have lacked you?
Summer gave us sweets, but autumn wrought
　　　　　　　　　　division?
　　Things were not lastly as firstly well
　　　　With us twain, you tell?
But all's closed now, despite Time's derision.

I see what you are doing: you are leading me on
　　To the spots we knew when we haunted here
　　　　　　　　　　together,
The waterfall, above which the mist-bow shone
　　At the then fair hour in the then fair weather,
And the cave just under, with a voice still so hollow
That it seems to call out to me from forty years ago,
　　When you were all aglow,
And not the thin ghost that I now fraily follow!

Ignorant of what there is flitting here to see,
    The waked birds preen and the seals flop lazily;
Soon you will have, Dear, to vanish from me,
    For the stars close their shutters and the
                                dawn whitens hazily.
Trust me, I mind not, though Life lours,
    The bringing me here; nay, bring me here again!
        I am just the same as when
Our days were a joy, and our paths through flowers.


THOMAS HARDY

*A Thunderstorm in Town*


She wore a 'terra-cotta' dress,
And we stayed, because of the pelting storm,
Within the hansom's dry recess,
Though the horse had stopped; yea, motionless
    We sat on, snug and warm.

Then the downpour ceased, to my sharp sad pain,
And the glass that had screened our forms before
Flew up, and out she sprang to her door:
I should have kissed her if the rain
    Had lasted a minute more.

# THOMAS HARDY

## *In the Vaulted Way*

In the vaulted way, where the passage turned
To the shadowy corner that none could see,
You paused for our parting, – plaintively:
Though overnight had come words that burned
My fond frail happiness out of me.

And then I kissed you, – despite my thought
That our spell must end when reflection came
On what you had deemed me, whose one long aim
Had been to serve you; that what I sought
Lay not in a heart that could breathe such blame.

But yet I kissed you: whereon you again
As of old kissed me. Why, why was it so?
Do you cleave to me after that light-tongued blow?
If you scorned me at eventide, how love then?
The thing is dark, Dear. I do not know.

THOMAS HARDY

## The Ballad-Singer

Sing, Ballad-singer, raise a hearty tune;
Make me forget that there was ever a one
I walked with in the meek light of the moon
    When the day's work was done.

Rhyme, Ballad-rhymer, start a country song;
Make me forget that she whom I loved well
Swore she would love me dearly, love me long,
    Then – what I cannot tell!

Sing, Ballad-singer, from your little book;
Make me forget those heart-breaks, achings, fears;
Make me forget her name, her sweet sweet look –
    Make me forget her tears.

THOMAS HARDY

## Two Lips

    I kissed them in fancy as I came
        Away in the morning glow:
I kissed them through the glass of her picture-frame:
        She did not know.

    I kissed them in love, in troth, in laughter,
        When she knew all; long so!
That I should kiss them in a shroud thereafter
        She did not know.

CHARLOTTE MEW

## *The Farmer's Bride*

Three summers since I chose a maid,
Too young maybe – but more's to do
At harvest-time than bide and woo.
    When us was wed she turned afraid
Of love and me and all things human;
Like the shut of a winter's day.
Her smile went out, and 'twadn't a woman –
    More like a little frightened fay.
        One night, in the Fall, she runned away.

'Out 'mong the sheep, her be,' they said,
'Should properly have been abed;
But sure enough she wadn't there
Lying awake with her wide brown stare.
So over seven-acre field and up-along across the down
We chased her, flying like a hare
Before our lanterns. To Church-Town
    All in a shiver and a scare
We caught her, fetched her home at last
    And turned the key upon her, fast.

She does the work about the house
As well as most, but like a mouse:
    Happy enough to chat and play
    With birds and rabbits and such as they,
    So long as menfolk keep away.
'Not near, not near!' her eyes beseech
When one of us comes within reach.
    The women say that beasts in stall
    Look round like children at her call.
    I've hardly heard her speak at all.

Shy as a leveret, swift as he,
Straight and slight as a young larch tree,
Sweet as the first wild violets, she,
To her wild self. But what to me?

The short days shorten and the oaks are brown,
   The blue smoke rises to the low grey sky,
One leaf in the still air falls slowly down,
   A magpie's spotted feathers lie
On the black earth spread white with rime,
The berries redden up to Christmas-time.
   What's Christmas-time without there be
   Some other in the house than we!

   She sleeps up in the attic there
   Alone, poor maid. 'Tis but a stair
Betwixt us. Oh! my God! the down,
The soft young down of her, the brown,
The brown of her – her eyes, her hair, her hair!

CHARLOTTE MEW

## Rooms

I remember rooms that have had their part
In the steady slowing down of the heart.
The room in Paris, the room at Geneva,
The little damp room with the seaweed smell,
And that ceaseless maddening sound of the tide –
   Rooms where for good or for ill, things died.
But there is the room where we two lie dead,
Though every morning we seem to wake,
     and might just as well seem to sleep again
As we shall somewhere in the other dustier,
              quieter bed
Out there – in the sun – in the rain.

CHARLOTTE MEW

## I So Liked Spring

I so liked Spring last year
   Because you were here; –
      The thrushes too –
Because it was these you so liked to hear –
      I so liked you.

This year's a different thing, –
     I'll not think of you.
But I'll like the Spring because it is simply Spring
     As the thrushes do.

ELINOR WYLIE

## *Wild Peaches*

### 1

When the world turns completely upside down
You say we'll emigrate to the Eastern Shore
Aboard a river-boat from Baltimore;
We'll live among wild peach trees, miles from town,
You'll wear a coonskin cap, and I a gown
Homespun, dyed butternut's dark gold colour.
Lost, like your lotus-eating ancestor,
We'll swim in milk and honey till we drown.

The winter will be short, the summer long,
The autumn amber-hued, sunny and hot,
Tasting of cider and of scuppernong;
All seasons sweet, but autumn best of all.
The squirrels in their silver fur will fall
Like falling leaves, like fruit, before your shot.

### 2

The autumn frosts will lie upon the grass
Like bloom on grapes of purple-brown and gold.
The misted early mornings will be cold;
The little puddles will be roofed with glass.
The sun, which burns from copper into brass,
Melts these at noon, and makes the boys unfold
Their knitted mufflers; full as they can hold
Fat pockets dribble chestnuts as they pass.

Peaches grow wild, and pigs can live in clover;
A barrel of salted herrings lasts a year;
The spring begins before the winter's over.
By February you may find the skins

Of garter snakes and water moccasins
Dwindled and harsh, dead-white and cloudy-clear.


### 3

When April pours the colours of a shell
Upon the hills, when every little creek
Is shot with silver from the Chesapeake
In shoals new-minted by the ocean swell,
When strawberries go begging, and the sleek
Blue plums lie open to the blackbird's beak,
We shall live well – we shall live very well.

The months between the cherries and the peaches
Are brimming cornucopias which spill
Fruits red and purple, sombre-bloomed and black;
Then, down rich fields and frosty river beaches
We'll trample bright persimmons, while you kill
Bronze partridge, speckled quail, and canvasback.


### 4

Down to the Puritan marrow of my bones
There's something in this richness that I hate.
I love the look, austere, immaculate,
Of landscapes drawn in pearly monotones.
There's something in my very blood that owns
Bare hills, cold silver on a sky of slate,
A thread of water, churned to milky spate
Streaming through slanted pastures fenced with stones.

I love those skies, thin blue or snowy gray,
Those fields sparse-planted, rendering meagre sheaves;
That spring, briefer than apple-blossom's breath,
Summer, so much too beautiful to stay,
Swift autumn, like a bonfire of leaves,
And sleepy winter, like the sleep of death.

### D. H. LAWRENCE

## Green

The dawn was apple-green,
The sky was green wine held up in the sun,
The moon was a golden petal between.

She opened her eyes, and green
They shone, clear like flowers undone
For the first time, now for the first time seen.


### D. H. LAWRENCE

## Rose of all the World

I am here myself; as though this heave of effort
At starting other life, fulfilled my own;
Rose-leaves that whirl in colour round a core
Of seed-specks kindled lately and softly blown

By all the blood of the rose-bush into being –
Strange, that the urgent will in me, to set
My mouth on hers in kisses, and so softly
To bring together two strange sparks, beget

Another life from our lives, so should send
The innermost fire of my own dim soul out-spinning
And whirling in blossom of flame and being upon me!
That my completion of manhood should be the
                                                          beginning

Another life from mine! For so it looks.
The seed is purpose, blossom accident.
The seed is all in all, the blossom lent
To crown the triumph of this new descent.

Is that it, woman? Does it strike you so?
The Great Breath blowing a tiny seed of fire
Fans out your petals for excess of flame,
Till all your being smokes with fine desire?

Or are we kindled, you and I, to be
One rose of wonderment upon the tree
Of perfect life, and is our possible seed
But the residuum of the ecstasy?

How will you have it? – the rose is all in all,
Or the ripe rose-fruits of the luscious fall?
The sharp begetting, or the child begot?
Our consummation matters, or does it not?

To me it seems the seed is just left over
From the red rose-flowers' fiery transience;
Just orts and slarts; berries that smoulder in the bush
Which burnt just now with marvellous immanence.

Blossom, my darling, blossom, be a rose
Of roses unchidden and purposeless; a rose
For rosiness only, without an ulterior motive;
For me it is more than enough if the flower unclose.

D. H. LAWRENCE

## Gloire de Dijon

When she rises in the morning
I linger to watch her;
She spreads the bath-cloth underneath the window
And the sunbeams catch her
Glistening white on the shoulders,
While down her sides the mellow
Golden shadow glows as
She stoops to the sponge, and her swung breasts
Sway like full-blown yellow
Gloire de Dijon roses.

She drips herself with water, and her shoulders
Glisten as silver, they crumple up
Like wet and falling roses, and I listen
For the sluicing of their rain-dishevelled petals.
In the window full of sunlight
Concentrates her golden shadow
Fold on fold, until it glows as
Mellow as the glory roses.

D. H. LAWRENCE

## Intimates

Don't you care for my love? she said bitterly.

I handed her the mirror, and said:
Please address these questions to the proper person!
Please make all requests to headquarters!
In all matters of emotional importance
please approach the supreme authority direct! –
So I handed her the mirror.
And she would have broken it over my head,
but she caught sight of her own reflection
and that held her spellbound for two seconds
while I fled.

## ROBERT BRIDGES

### *Melancholia*

The sickness of desire, that in dark days
Looks on the imagination of despair,
Forgetteth man, and stinteth God his praise;
Nor but in sleep findeth a cure for care.
Incertainty that once gave scope to dream
Of laughing enterprise and glory untold,
Is now a blackness that no stars redeem,
A wall of terror in a night of cold.

Fool! thou that hast impossibly desired
And now impatiently despairest, see
How nought is changed: Joy's wisdom is attired
Splended for others' eyes if not for thee:
Not love or beauty or youth from earth is fled:
If they delite thee not, 'tis thou art dead.

ROBERT BRIDGES

## *For Beauty being the Best of All We Know*

For beauty being the best of all we know
Sums up the unsearchable and secret aims
Of nature, and on joys whose earthly names
Were never told can form and sense bestow;
And man has sped his instinct to outgo
The step of science; and against her shames
Imagination stakes out heavenly claims,
Building a tower above the head of woe.
Nor is there fairer work for beauty found
Than that she win in nature her release
From all the woes that in the world abound;
Nay with his sorrow may his love increase,
If from man's greater need beauty redound,
And claim his tears for homage of his peace.

ROBERT BRIDGES

## *My Delight and Thy Delight*

My delight and thy delight
Walking, like two angels white,
In the gardens of the night:
My desire and thy desire
Twinning to a tongue of fire,
Leaping live, and laughing higher;
Thro' the everlasting strife
In the mystery of life.
Love, from whom the world begun,
Hath the secret of the sun.
Love can tell and love alone,
Whence the million stars are strewn,
Why each atom knows its own,
How, in spite of woe and death,
Gay is life, and sweet is breath:
This he taught us, this we knew,
Happy in his science true,
Hand in hand as we stood
'Neath the shadows of the wood,
Heart to heart as we lay
In the dawning of the day.

KAHLIL GIBRAN

## *On Marriage*
FROM *The Prophet*

You were born together, and together you shall
 be for evermore.
You shall be together when the white wings of
 death scatter your days.
Ay, you shall be together even in the silent memory
 of God.
But let there be spaces in your togetherness,
And let the winds of heavens dance between you.

Love one another, but make not a bond of love:
Let it rather be a moving sea between the shores
 of your souls.
Fill each other's cup but drink not from one cup.
Give one another of your bread but eat not from
 the same loaf.
Sing and dance together and be joyous, but let
 each one of you be alone.
Even as the strings of a lute are alone though
 they quiver with the same music.

Give your hearts, but not into each other's keeping.
For only the hand of Life can contain your hearts.
And stand together yet not too near together:
For the pillars of the temple stand apart,
And the oak tree and the cypress grow not in
 each other's shadow.

HAROLD HART CRANE

### Carrier Letter

My hands have not touched water since
                                        your hands, –
No; – nor my lips freed laughter since 'farewell'.
And with the day, distance again expands
Between us, voiceless as an uncoiled shell.

Yet, – much follows, much endures . . .
                                Trust birds alone:
A dove's wings clung about my heart last night
With surging gentleness; and the blue stone
Set in the tryst-ring has but worn more bright.

CHRISTOPHER BRENNAN

## Because She would Ask Me
## Why I Loved Her

If questioning would make us wise
No eyes would ever gaze in eyes;
If all our tale were told in speech
No mouths would wander each to each.

Were spirits free from mortal mesh
And love not bound in hearts of flesh
No aching breasts would yearn to meet
And find their ecstasy complete.

For who is there that lives and knows
The secret powers by which he grows?
Were knowledge all, what were our need
To thrill and faint and sweetly bleed?

Then seek not, sweet, the 'If' and 'Why'
I love you now until I die.
For I must love because I live
And life in me is what you give.

CHRISTOPHER BRENNAN

## *I am Shut Out of Mine Own Heart*

I am shut out of mine own heart
because my love is far from me,
nor in the wonders have I part
that fill its hidden empery:

The wildwood of adventurous thought
and lands of dawn my dream had won,
the riches out of Faery brought
are buried with our bridal sun.

And I am in a narrow place,
and all its little streets are cold,
because the absence of her face
has robb'd the sullen air of gold.

My home is in a broader day:
at times I catch it glistening
thro' the dull gate, a flower'd play
and odour of undying spring:

The long days that I lived alone,
sweet madness of the springs I miss'd,
are shed beyond, and thro' them blown
clear laughter, and my lips are kiss'd:

And here, from mine own joy apart,
I wait the turning of the key: –
I am shut out of mine own heart
because my love is far from me.

SARA TEASDALE

## I Love You

When April bends above me
And finds me fast asleep,
Dust need not keep the secret
A live heart died to keep.

When April tells the thrushes,
The meadow-larks will know,
And pipe the three words lightly
To all the winds that blow.

Above his roof the swallows,
In notes like far-blown rain,
Will tell the little sparrow
Beside his window-pane.

O sparrow, little sparrow,
When I am fast asleep,
Then tell my love the secret
That I have died to keep.

A. E. HOUSMAN

## The Rainy Pleiads Wester

The rainy Pleiads wester,
  Orion plunges prone,
The stroke of midnight ceases
  And I lie down alone.

The rainy Pleiads wester,
  And seek beyond the sea
The head that I shall dream of
  That will not dream of me.


A. E. HOUSMAN

## FROM *A Shropshire Lad*

Oh, when I was in love with you,
  Then I was clean and brave,
And miles around the wonder grew
  How well did I behave.

And now the fancy passes by,
  And nothing will remain,
And miles around they'll say that I
  Am quite myself again.

A. E. HOUSMAN

FROM *A Shropshire Lad*

When I was one-and-twenty
   I heard a wise man say,
'Give crowns and pounds and guineas
   But not your heart away;
Give pearls away and rubies
   But keep your fancy free.'
But I was one-and-twenty,
   No use to talk to me.

When I was one-and-twenty
   I heard him say again,
'The heart out of the bosom
   Was never given in vain;
'Tis paid with sighs a plenty
   And sold for endless rue.'
And I am two-and-twenty,
   And oh, 'tis true, 'tis true.

## The Song of Wandering Aengus

I went out to the hazel wood,
Because a fire was in my head,
And cut and peeled a hazel wand,
And hooked a berry to a thread;
And when white moths were on the wing,
And moth-like stars were flickering out,
I dropped the berry in a stream
And caught a little silver trout.

When I had laid it on the floor
I went to blow the fire a-flame,
But something rustled on the floor,
And someone called me by my name:
It had become a glimmering girl
With apple blossom in her hair
Who called me by my name and ran
And faded through the brightening air.

Though I am old with wandering
Through hollow lands and hilly lands,
I will find out where she has gone,
And kiss her lips and take her hands;
And walk among long dappled grass,
And pluck till time and times are done,
The silver apples of the moon,
The golden apples of the sun.

## The Folly of being Comforted

One that is ever kind said yesterday:
'Your well-beloved's hair has threads of grey,
And little shadows come about her eyes;
Time can but make it easier to be wise
Though now it seems impossible, and so
All that you need is patience.'
Heart cries, 'No,
I have not a crumb of comfort, not a grain.
Time can but make her beauty over again:
Because of that great nobleness of hers
The fire that stirs about her, when she stirs,
Burns but more clearly. O she had not these ways
When all the wild Summer was in her gaze.'
Heart! O heart! if she'd but turn her head,
You'd know the folly of being comforted.

### W. B. YEATS

## *For Anne Gregory*

'Never shall a young man,
Thrown into despair
By those great honey-coloured
Ramparts at your ear,
Love you for yourself alone
And not your yellow hair.'

'But I can get a hair-dye
And set such colour there,
Brown, or black, or carrot,
That young men in despair
May love me for myself alone
And not my yellow hair.'

'I heard an old religious man
But yesternight declare
That he had found a text to prove
That only God, my dear,
Could love you for yourself alone
And not your yellow hair.'

W. B. YEATS

## When You are Old

When you are old and grey and full of sleep,
And nodding by the fire, take down this book,
And slowly read, and dream of the soft look
Your eyes had once, and of their shadows deep;

How many loved your moments of glad grace,
And loved your beauty with love false or true,
But one man loved the pilgrim soul in you,
And loved the sorrows of your changing face;

And bending down beside the glowing bars,
Murmur, a little sadly, how Love fled
And paced upon the mountains overhead
And hid his face amid a crowd of stars.

W. B. YEATS

## A Drinking Song

Wine comes in at the mouth
And love comes in at the eye;
That's all we shall know for truth
Before we grow old and die.
I lift the glass to my mouth,
I look at you, and I sigh.

*Love Poetry*

W. B. YEATS

## Lullaby

Beloved, may your sleep be sound
That have found it where you fed.
What were all the world's alarms
To mighty Paris when he found
Sleep upon a golden bed
That first dawn in Helen's arms?

Sleep, beloved, such a sleep
As did that wild Tristram know
When, the potion's work being done,
Roe could run or doe could leap
Under oak and beechen bough,
Roe could leap or doe could run;

Such a sleep and sound as fell
Upon Eurotas' grassy bank
When the holy bird, that there
Accomplished his predestined will,
From the limbs of Leda sank
But not from her protecting care.

## W. B. YEATS

### *Brown Penny*

I whispered, 'I am too young,'
And then, 'I am old enough';
Wherefore I threw a penny
To find out if I might love.
'Go and love, go and love, young man,
If the lady be young and fair.'
Ah, penny, brown penny, brown penny,
I am looped in the loops of her hair.

O love is the crooked thing,
There is nobody wise enough
To find out all that is in it,
For he would be thinking of love
Till the stars had run away
And the shadows eaten the moon.
Ah, penny, brown penny, brown penny,
One cannot begin it too soon.

### W. B. YEATS

## *Never Give All the Heart*

Never give all the heart, for love
Will hardly seem worth thinking of
To passionate women if it seem
Certain, and they never dream
That it fades out from kiss to kiss;
For everything that's lovely is
But a brief, dreamy, kind delight.
O never give the heart outright,
For they, for all smooth lips can say,
Have given their hearts up to the play.
And who could play it well enough
If deaf and dumb and blind with love?
He that made this knows all the cost,
For he gave all his heart and lost.

## W. B. YEATS

### *He Wishes for the Cloths of Heaven*

Had I the heavens' embroidered cloths,
Enwrought with golden and silver light,
The blue and the dim and the dark cloths
Of night and light and the half-light,
I would spread the cloths under your feet:
But I, being poor, have only my dreams;
I have spread my dreams under your feet;
Tread softly because you tread on my dreams.


## W. B. YEATS

### *Down by the Salley Gardens*

Down by the salley gardens
   my love and I did meet;
She passed the salley gardens
   with little snow-white feet.
She bid me take love easy,
   as the leaves grow on the tree;
But I, being young and foolish,
   with her would not agree.

In a field by the river
   my love and I did stand,
And on my leaning shoulder
   she laid her snow-white hand.
She bid me take life easy,
   as the grass grows on the weirs;
But I was young and foolish,
   and now am full of tears.

W. B. YEATS

## After Long Silence

Speech after long silence; it is right,
All other lovers being estranged or dead,
Unfriendly lamplight hid under its shade,
The curtains drawn upon unfriendly night,
That we descant and yet again descant
Upon the supreme theme of Art and Song:
Bodily decrepitude is wisdom; young
We loved each other and were ignorant.

## Poets' Biographies

### SIR EDWIN ARNOLD (1832–1904)

Arnold was a poet and journalist. He was primarily interested in interpreting Eastern thought for an English audience, and is best-known for his epic poem *The Light of Asia*, which centres on the life and teaching of the Buddha.

### MATTHEW ARNOLD (1822–1888)

Arnold was a poet, critic and inspector of schools. His work as the latter gave him the opportunity to travel widely in the early years of the railway, and as a result he became well acquainted with provincial England. He was greatly interested in social and theological issues, and his poetry is considered by many to be an accurate barometer of the intellectual concerns of his time.

### WILLIAM BLAKE (1757–1827)

Blake never achieved fame during his lifetime and made a living as an engraver and illustrator. He was a radical thinker and nonconformist (Thomas Paine and Mary Wollstonecraft were among his contemporaries) and is now recognised as one of the most important of England's Romantic poets.

### ANNE BRADSTREET (1612–1672)

Bradstreet, a Puritan and one of America's most important early poets, emigrated to New England in 1630. Much of her poetry reflects her struggle to honour her religious belief while expressing her emotions and individuality.

### CHRISTOPHER BRENNAN (1870–1932)

Brennan was a scholar as well as a poet, but lost his academic post after he turned to drink following his divorce. He died in poverty, but is now among Australia's most influential and important poets.

### ROBERT BRIDGES (1844–1930)

Bridges studied medicine and then worked as a doctor until his early retirement as a result of lung disease in 1882. He had already been writing seriously, but was now able to devote himself almost exclusively to his poetry. He served as Poet Laureate from 1913 to 1930.

### EMILY BRONTË (1818–1848)

Emily Brontë is the sister of novelists Charlotte Brontë and Anne Brontë. She herself is best known as the author of *Wuthering Heights* but is also an accomplished and highly acclaimed poet. She died at the age of thirty, just a year after *Wuthering Heights* was published.

### RUPERT BROOKE (1887–1915)

Brooke's early poems were inspired by love and by nature, but it was after he joined the Royal Navy in 1914 that he became a truly celebrated poet. His idealistic and patriotic poems reflected the mood during the early years of the First World War, and when he died of blood-poisoning at the age of twenty-seven he was already considered a national hero.

### ELIZABETH BARRETT BROWNING (1806–1861)

In 1844 Elizabeth Barrett published a collection of poetry, *Poems*, and it was after reading this that Robert Browning was moved to write to her. Thus began a prolific and heartfelt exchange of letters and a justly famous literary love affair. They married against the wishes of her father and moved to Italy, where they had a son, Robert Wideman Browning. She was probably the most widely admired of the Victorian woman poets – both for the beauty of her poetry and the strength and independence of her opinions.

### ROBERT BROWNING (1812–1889)

Browning only ever wanted to devote himself to poetry and remained dependent on his family until he married Elizabeth Barrett in 1846. For much of their marriage, Elizabeth was the more obviously successful of the two, but by the time he died in 1889 (she died in 1861) he had achieved significant critical acclaim. He is now considered one of the most important of the Victorian poets.

### ROBERT BURNS (1759–1796)

Burns was born into a farming family, and much of his poetry celebrates farming life, local culture and traditions and reflects the concerns of a country going through a period of transition and turning increasingly away from farming and towards industry. He is widely regarded as Scotland's national poet.

## LORD BYRON (GEORGE GORDON) (1788–1824)

Byron was, in many ways, the ideal Romantic hero, and he was as popular in his day as he is now. In the words of Lady Caroline Lamb, he was 'mad, bad and dangerous to know', and his romantic adventures and unconventional ideas informed his often passionate and beautiful poetry. He was on his way to join the fight for Greek independence when he died, aged thirty-six, of malaria.

## THOMAS CAMPION (1567–1620)

Campion was a poet, a composer and a physician. He continued working as a physician right up until his death in 1620, but this did not stop him being a prolific poet and composer, and achieving considerable literary and musical fame during his lifetime. It is thought that he died of the plague.

## THOMAS CAREW (1595–1640)

Carew (pronounced 'Carey') was a poet at the court of Charles I and a friend of both John Donne and Ben Jonson. With his move towards celebrating and glorifying both King and court in his poetry and away from traditional subjects such as religion and philosophy, he became one of the new 'Cavalier Poets' of the seventeenth century.

## CATULLUS (c.84–c.54BC)

Very little is known about the Roman poet Catullus, whose full name was Gaius Valerius Catullus. He was a popular and successful poet during his lifetime (though many readers were shocked by his explicit references) and then found a new and appreciative audience when he was rediscovered in the fourteenth century.

## GEOFFREY CHAUCER (c.1343–1400)

By writing in English, Chaucer played a crucial role in showing that the vernacular, rather than French and Latin, could be a literary language. He was a diplomat and a scientist as well as a writer, and he is – almost unarguably – the greatest English poet of the Middle Ages. Significantly, he was the first poet to be buried in Poet's corner in Westminster Abbey.

## JOHN CLARE (1793–1864)

Much of Clare's poetry is concerned with the natural world and celebrations of the English countryside. Clare suffered from delusions, and in 1837 he was certified insane and admitted to a lunatic asylum, from which he discharged himself and walked the eighty miles home four years later. He was then admitted to another asylum, where he stayed until his death in 1864.

## MARY COLERIDGE (1861–1907)

Mary Coleridge was a novelist, critic and poet. She was the great-grandniece of Samuel Taylor Coleridge, and her family was extremely well connected in the literary world – Alfred, Lord Tennyson, Robert Browning and Holman Hunt were all family friends. Coleridge published her poetry under the pseudonym Anodos, a name she took from a character in the novels of George MacDonald.

### SAMUEL TAYLOR COLERIDGE (1772–1834)

Coleridge was a highly influential poet, thinker and critic, and, together with his great friend William Wordsworth, he is credited with founding the Romantic movement in England. The pair co-wrote *Lyrical Ballads* which became a key text for the movement. Sadly, Coleridge became increasingly dependent on opium in his later years, and this addiction most probably led to his death of heart failure at the age of sixty-one.

### WILLIAM CONGREVE (1670–1729)

Congreve was a poet and playwright, whose early comedies were immediately successful. Sadly, public taste soon turned against him, and after this promising start he never reached the same heights of popularity again. But his plays – and his poetry – have stood the test of time, and he is still thought of as one of the great writers of the Restoration period.

### ABRAHAM COWLEY (1618–1667)

Cowley published his first collection of poetry at the age of 15. His life as a poet and essayist was disrupted by the Civil War, which saw him siding with the Royalists. He spent twelve years in exile in Paris, but then returned to England – and to his post at Cambridge University – after the Restoration of the English monarchy.

### GEORGE CRABBE (1754–1832)

Crabbe started out as a surgeon but then moved to London to make his way as a poet, and it was largely thanks to the support of the author Edmund Burke that he was able to build a successful career, both as a poet and as a clergyman (a role he found far more compatible with poetry than that of surgeon). Much of Crabbe's poetry speaks of the everyday lives of ordinary people, and this set him apart from many of his contemporaries.

### HAROLD HART CRANE (1899–1932)

The American modernist Harold Hart Crane is now considered one of the most significant poets of his generation. But his life and career were beset by financial instability and by alcohol, and a move from New York to Paris didn't alleviate his problems. His death at sea after jumping from a steamship was most likely suicide.

### EMILY DICKINSON (1830–1886)

Dickinson was famously reclusive and shunned social contact. Very few of her poems were published during her lifetime, and it was only after her death that the true extent of her talent was discovered. She broke new ground in freeing expression from traditional forms and is now considered one of America's finest poets.

### JOHN DONNE (1572–1631)

One of the most important of the metaphysical poets, Donne was born into a devout Catholic family. He was briefly imprisoned for marrying Anne More, great-niece of Thomas More, against her father's wishes, and the couple – and their many children – lived in poverty for several years before Donne finally acceded to James I's wishes and became a cleric in the Church of England.

## ERNEST DOWSON (1867–1900)

A writer of novels, short stories and poems, Dowson was a friend of Oscar Wilde and was associated with the Decadent movement. Tragically, he died of excessive drinking at the age of thirty-two.

## MICHAEL DRAYTON (1563–1631)

Not very much is known about the early life of Michael Drayton, but it is likely that he was of humble origin, was born in Warwickshire and at some point moved to London. There he moved in literary circles and was a favourite at Elizabeth I's court, but he fell out of royal favour when James I came to power.

## WILLIAM DRUMMOND OF HAWTHORNDEN
## (1585–1649)

The Scottish poet William Drummond became the laird of Hawthornden Castle at the age of twenty-four, an entitlement which allowed him to give up his law studies and devote himself to poetry. He was friends with many major literary figures of the time, including Michael Drayton and Ben Jonson.

## JOHN DRYDEN (1631–1700)

Dryden was a poet, playwright, translator and critic, and a major literary figure in England during the Restoration. He became Poet Laureate in 1668, but when William III became king in 1688 Dryden refused allegiance, and he therefore has the distinction of being the only poet ever to have been dismissed from the post.

## PAUL LAURENCE DUNBAR (1872–1906)

Dunbar's parents were freed slaves, and he was one of the very first African-Americans to make his name as a poet. He wrote poems in standard English and in African-American dialect, and his work was ground breaking in its informal tone and lively language. He died of tuberculosis at the age of thirty-three.

## SIR EDWARD DYER (1543–1607)

Dyer was a friend of Sir Philip Sidney and of Edmund Spenser. He was a courtier as well as a poet, and Elizabeth I employed him on various foreign missions, knighting him for his services in 1596. Sadly, very little of his poetry has survived.

## RALPH WALDO EMERSON (1803–1882)

Emerson was highly influential in the intellectual circles of nineteenth-century America and achieved considerable fame as a lecturer and orator. He spoke out against slavery and was a great believer in the power of the individual.

## SIR RICHARD FANSHAWE (1608–1666)

Fanshawe was a diplomat, politician, poet, and a translator from Italian, Latin, Portuguese and Spanish. He was on the side of the Royalists during the English Civil War and served Charles II, both in battle and in exile, and was then involved in many foreign missions following the Restoration of the monarchy.

## ANNE FINCH, COUNTESS OF WINCHILSEA
### (1661–1720)

One of the earliest women poets to be published in England, Finch spoke out against the restrictions imposed upon women and the misogynistic attitudes of the time. But her poetry also had a very personal side to it, and she frequently speaks of the supportive and happy nature of her marriage – as in 'A Letter to Daphnis' included here.

## EDWARD FITZGERALD (1809–1883)

Fitzgerald was a poet, writer, translator and student of Orientalism; he was from a wealthy family and therefore able to devote himself to his literary work. He is best known as the translator of the *Rubáiyát of Omar Khayyám*.

## JOHN FLETCHER (1579–1625)

Fletcher was one of the most highly regarded and influential Jacobean writers in his day. He wrote more than fifty plays, and his standing as a playwright equalled that of Shakespeare. But, by the beginning of the eighteenth century, Shakespeare's plays had become the more frequently performed, and Fletcher's reputation has never fully recovered – his plays are now very rarely performed.

## BENJAMIN FRANKLIN (1706–1790)

Franklin frequently wrote under pseudonyms, and his success as an author is now totally eclipsed by his other achievements; he was a key figure in the American Enlightenment – he made important discoveries in the field of physics – and was, most importantly, one of the Founding Fathers of the United States.

## KAHLIL GIBRAN (1883–1931)

Gibran was a Lebanese artist and writer who moved to the United States as a young man. He wrote in both Arabic and English, and in the Arab world his poetry was ground breaking in its departure from classical tradition. In the English-speaking world, his reputation rests chiefly on his book *The Prophet*, which is now one of the best-selling poetry books of all time.

## OLIVER GOLDSMITH (1730–1774)

Goldsmith was an Anglo-Irish novelist, playwright and poet. His literary work brought him to the attention of Samuel Johnson and other leading writers of his day, but his dissolute lifestyle and addiction to gambling meant that he was often in debt. He is now best known for his play *The Vicar of Wakefield*.

## GEORGE GRANVILLE, 1ST BARON LANSDOWNE (1666–1735)

Granville was a poet, playwright and politician. He was a friend of John Dryden's, and his plays achieved some success during his lifetime but are rarely performed today.

## THOMAS HARDY (1840–1928)

Hardy is now probably best known as a novelist, but in fact he considered himself first and foremost a poet. He was born in Dorset and spent much of his life there, and his native countryside was always an important element in his work. His career straddled two centuries – and two different eras – and his modern style was to be a great influence on British twentieth-century poetry.

### SIR JOHN HARINGTON (1561–1612)

Harington was a translator, author, courtier and great wit, but his claim to fame is as the inventor of the flush toilet. He was a member of the court of both Elizabeth I and James I, but the risqué nature of his poetry meant that he frequently caused offence, and, during Elizabeth's reign, he spent several years banished from the court.

### GEORGE HERBERT (1593–1633)

The Welsh-born Herbert was one of the most influential of the Metaphysical poets, and he is well known for his deeply religious poetry. His family was both wealthy and well connected, and Herbert was probably destined for high political office, but his true interest had always been the church and in 1630, only three years before he died, he became a priest.

### ROBERT HERRICK (1591–1674)

Herrick's poetry speaks of making the most of life and enjoying the experience of love, but his contemporaries were more receptive to the complex poetry of the metaphysical poets and he only really achieved popularity in the nineteenth century. Since then his reputation has prospered, and he is now recognised as one of the foremost poets of the seventeenth century.

*Love Poetry*

## HORACE (65–8 BC)

Quintus Horatius Flaccus was the most celebrated Roman lyric poet during the reign of Augustus. He is usually known simply as 'Horace' and is best known for his Odes. He was a satirist and literary critic, as well as a poet.

## A. E. HOUSMAN (1859–1936)

Alfred Edward Housman was two very different things: a classical scholar and the author of evocative and highly romantic poetry. The march of time and the inevitability of death were major themes in his poetry, and his cycle of poems entitled *A Shropshire Lad*, with its evocation of doomed youth and the beauty of the English countryside, has become an oft-recited and much-loved classic.

## LEIGH HUNT (1784–1859)

Hunt was a critic and essayist as well as a poet, and, along with his brother, he spent two years in prison for slandering the Prince Regent. As a poet, he was a key figure in the Romantic movement, although he never quite achieved the critical acclaim and popularity of his friends and fellow poets Shelley and Byron.

## BEN JONSON (1572–1637)

Jonson was a dramatist as well as a poet, and his first important play, *Every Man in his Humour*, included William Shakespeare in its cast. King James I conferred royal patronage upon him, and by the time of his death in 1637 he was known as one of the great playwrights and poets of his age.

## JOHN KEATS (1795–1821)

Keats trained as a doctor, but he soon gave up medicine in order to devote himself to poetry. He died of tuberculosis at the age of twenty-five, but the many poetic masterpieces he produced in his short life have ensured his standing as one of the most admired and widely read figures of the Romantic movement.

## OMAR KHAYYÁM (1048–1131)

Khayyám was a Persian mathematician, philosopher, astronomer and poet, but of his many achievements it is the *Rubáiyát of Omar Khayyám* for which he is best known and which, following Edward Fitzgerald's translation, made him famous in the West.

## WALTER SAVAGE LANDOR (1775–1864)

Landor was a serious classicist and writer, as comfortable writing in Latin as in English. He was well respected by his contemporaries and his work was critically acclaimed, but his hot temper frequently landed him in trouble, and his writings were often considered libellous. It was a career beset by misfortune, which perhaps overshadowed his brilliance.

## D. H. LAWRENCE (1885–1930)

David Herbert Lawrence was a poet, novelist, playwright, critic and artist. The negative effects of industrialisation on the human spirit were a major theme in his work, and one which resulted in persecution and censorship. But after his death the literary importance and moral seriousness of his work were finally appreciated, and he is now considered one of Britain's great modernist writers.

## EDWARD LEAR (1812–1888)

Despite very poor health, Lear successfully combined work as an artist and as a writer. But it is for his limericks and other nonsense poetry that he is best known, and his verbal inventiveness and imagination – very much in evidence in *The Owl and the Pussycat* – have ensured his lasting popularity.

## RICHARD LOVELACE (1618–1657)

Lovelace was one of the Cavalier poets and a soldier. He fought for the Royalist cause during the English Civil War, and his allegiance to Charles I resulted in more than one period of imprisonment. He spent his final years in poverty and died in a London slum at the age of thirty-nine.

## CHRISTOPHER MARLOWE (1564–1593)

Marlowe was born in the same year as Shakespeare, and – like Shakespeare – he became a celebrated dramatist and poet. But his life was mired in suspicions of heresy and atheism, and he was arrested at the age of twenty-nine on a charge of blasphemy. He was killed under mysterious circumstances soon after, and his death is still the subject of numerous conspiracy theories.

## PHILIP BOURKE MARSTON (1850–1887)

Marston, who was partially blind from an early age, was born into a well-connected family; Charles

Dickens, the Rossettis and A. C. Swinburne would all have been visitors to the family home. The increasingly sorrowful tone of much of his poetry probably stemmed from the shock of losing many of his close friends and family in quick succession.

### ANDREW MARVELL (1621–1678)

During his lifetime, Marvell's reputation was as a satirist and pamphleteer, rather than as one of his century's pre-eminent poets, and his claim to fame was principally for attacking the corruption of Charles II's court. But by the twentieth century his witty and vibrant poetry had established him as one of the great Metaphysical poets, alongside John Donne and George Herbert.

### GEORGE MEREDITH (1828–1909)

Meredith is perhaps better known as a novelist than as a poet, but even his novels were never quite as successful as he would have liked. He was influential within literary circles and his friends included Dante Gabriel Rossetti, A. C. Swinburne and Robert Louis Stevenson.

### CHARLOTTE MEW (1869–1928)

Mew's life was rather a tragic one, and the sadness and struggles she experienced became themes in her poetry and short stories. She was one of seven children, but three siblings died in childhood, and another two both spent most of their lives in mental institutions. Mew herself committed suicide after falling into a depression following the death of her last remaining sister from cancer.

*Love Poetry*

## ALICE MEYNELL (1847–1922)

Meynell was a writer, editor, journalist and critic. In later life she became a suffragist and a leading figure in the Women Writers' Suffrage League.

## JOHN MILTON (1608–1674)

Milton was one of the great historians and pamphleteers of the seventeenth century, and he was a man of great and lasting influence in what was a time of considerable political strife and civil war, despite his failing eyesight and eventual blindness. But of course he is also the author of arguably the most famous epic poem in the English language, *Paradise Lost*.

## THOMAS MOORE (1779–1852)

The son of a Dublin grocer, Moore travelled to London in 1799 where he became a popular poet, singer, balladeer and entertainer. Famously, his close friend Lord Byron entrusted him with his memoirs after his death, and Moore burnt the diaries, apparently in an effort to protect his friend. Moore is still considered Ireland's national poet.

## OVID (43BC–AD17/18)

Ovid was a Roman poet who spent much of his life far from Rome on the island of Tomis, banished there by the emperor Augustus. The reasons for this exile have never been definitively known, but Ovid wrote that his crime was 'a poem and a mistake'. His full name was Publius Ovidius Naso.

## WILFRED OWEN (1893–1918)

Wilfred Owen, one of the most accomplished of Britain's First World War poets and a great friend of Siegfried Sassoon, composed most of his poems between August 1917 and September 1918. He was killed in action just one week before the Armistice in November 1918.

## COVENTRY PATMORE (1823–1896)

From an early age Patmore was encouraged in his literary efforts by his father, a novelist and editor. Patmore's interest in both art and literature soon brought him into contact with the Pre-Raphaelites, and his circle of friends and acquaintances included Dante Gabriel Rossetti, William Holman Hunt, John Ruskin and John Singer Sargent.

## PETRONIUS (c.AD27–66)

Gaius Petronius Arbiter was a Roman courtier and satirist during the reign of Nero. Apart from this, very little is known about his life.

## KATHERINE PHILIPS (1632–1664)

Philips was an Anglo-Welsh poet and translator, and one of the first women in England to become renowned as a woman of letters. She was at the centre of a literary group called the Society of Friendship, and many of her poems celebrate her love for her women friends. She is sometimes known as 'the English Sappho'.

## EDGAR ALLAN POE (1809–1849)

Poe's first work to be published was a book of poems, and he subsequently achieved fame for his poem 'The Raven'. But he was of course also a critic and a writer of short stories; his tales of mystery and horror laid the foundations for the modern detective story, and his significant influence on American literature is felt across many genres.

## ALEXANDER POPE (1688–1744)

Pope, the son of a Catholic linen draper, was crippled while still a child by a form of tuberculosis that affected his spine. His translations of Homer enabled him to achieve financial independence, and his own work soon brought him success – especially his most famous poem, *The Rape of the Lock*.

## SIR WALTER RALEGH (c.1552–1618)

Sir Walter Ralegh (also spelt 'Raleigh') was an explorer, poet and a favourite courtier of Elizabeth I. He is perhaps best known for his voyages to the New World, and is credited with introducing both tobacco and potatoes to England. Under James I his fortunes changed, and he was accused of treason, imprisoned in the Tower of London and executed.

## THOMAS RANDOLPH (1605–1635)

Randolph was a poet and dramatist, whose grasp of comedy made his plays immediately successful; they were highly praised by Ben Jonson and other contemporaries. Sadly, Randolph's career was cut short by his death at the age of twenty-nine.

## CHRISTINA ROSSETTI (1830–1894)

Rossetti – along with Elizabeth Barrett Browning – was one of England's most admired nineteenth-century women poets. She was the sister of Dante Gabriel Rossetti, and her poetry, in its use of symbolism and medieval elements, has much in common with the work of the Pre-Raphaelite Brotherhood, though she never identified herself with the group.

## DANTE GABRIEL ROSSETTI (1828–1882)

Rossetti was a poet, translator, illustrator and painter, and the brother of the poet Christina Rossetti. He was one of the founders of the Pre-Raphaelite Brotherhood and had a great influence on poetry and art in the latter half of the nineteenth century.

## SAPPHO
### (Early Seventh Century BC)

Sappho was a Greek lyric poet who lived on the island of Lesbos. Much of her writing has been lost and we know her only through fragments of her verses, many of which focus on emotions between women.

## SIR WALTER SCOTT (1771–1832)

Scott's fame reached far beyond his native Scotland, and he was perhaps the first truly international author, with readers across the world. He was a poet before he became a novelist, and poetry, rather than fiction, was where his heart lay. But nowadays he is best known as the author of the highly popular *Waverley Novels*.

## SIR CHARLES SEDLEY (1639–1701)

Sedley was a dramatist, translator and politician who became, at the end of his career, Speaker of the House of Commons. He was, however, most famous for his wit, and for his rakish and dissolute behaviour.

## WILLIAM SHAKESPEARE (1564–1616)

As a playwright and poet, Shakespeare's fame is unrivalled. He married Anne Hathaway when he was eighteen – she was eight years his senior – but they lived apart for many years. It is thought that some of his sonnets were addressed to a young man, while others expressed his love for a married woman (the 'Dark Lady').

## PERCY BYSSHE SHELLEY (1792–1822)

Shelley's is now considered one of England's great Romantic poets, but his verse was never fully appreciated in his lifetime. His views were as radical as his poetry, and he was expelled from Oxford University after publishing a pamphlet entitled 'The Necessity of Atheism'. In 1816 he married Mary Wollstonecraft, the author (as Mary Shelley) of *Frankenstein*. He drowned off the coast of Italy at the age of twenty-nine.

## SIR PHILIP SIDNEY (1554–1586)

Sidney was a militant protestant and courtier, and one of the most important poets of the Elizabethan age. As a patron of the arts, he was a great supporter of young poets, and especially of Edmund Spenser. He died after being injured while fighting for the Protestant cause against the Spanish.

## EDMUND SPENSER (1552–1599)

Spenser was one of the most important poets of the Elizabethan age, and part of a new literary renaissance which attempted to give England the kind of national literature which it had so far lacked. He was greatly influenced by the classical poets, as well as by more recent religious poetry from the Continent and by Englands's greatest medieval poet, Geoffrey Chaucer.

## SIR JOHN SUCKLING (1609–1642)

Suckling was born into a wealthy family and inherited a fortune at the age of seventeen. He was known for his gaiety and wit, traits that went hand-in-hand with being a Cavalier poet. His political escapades in later life – he was involved in trying to rescue the Earl of Trafford from the Tower of London – were not successful, and he fled to Paris, where he committed suicide the following year. Suckling is apparently the inventor of the card game cribbage.

## A. C. SWINBURNE (1837–1909)

Algernon Charles Swinburne was a poet, novelist, playwright and critic. He rebelled against many of the conservative values and constraints of the Victorian age, and at the time his poetry was known as much for its sometimes shocking subject-matter as for its lyric beauty and power.

## SARA TEASDALE (1884–1933)

The American poet Sara Teasdale was born and brought up in Missouri and later moved to New York City. Her classical style belies the passionate nature of her lyrics, and beauty, love and death are recurrent themes in her poetry. She divorced in 1929 and, suffering from both depression and poor physical health, committed suicide in 1933.

### ALFRED, LORD TENNYSON (1809–1892)

Queen Victoria and Prince Albert were great admirers of Tennyson, and he was appointed Poet Laureate in 1850. He held the post until his death in 1892, and there has been no longer-serving Poet Laureate before or since. In many ways, he is a quintessentially Victorian poet, and he was as popular during his lifetime as he is now.

### EDWARD THOMAS (1878–1917)

For much of his career, Thomas was a writer of prose rather than poetry, but it is for his poems that he is chiefly remembered. He enlisted as a soldier in the First World War in 1915, and was killed in action during the Battle of Arras in 1917.

### EDMUND WALLER (1606–1687)

A poet and a politician, Waller was a member of Parliament during the political unrest of the 1640s. In 1643 he narrowly avoided death after being involved in a conspiracy against parliament, a development which became known as 'Waller's Plot'; on his arrest, he had quickly confessed, betraying his fellow conspirators. In his poetry, Waller rejected the intellectual concerns of the Metaphysical poets and favoured a more refined, urbane style. He is credited with paving the way for the heroic couplet in English poetry.

### WILLIAM WALSH (1662–1708)

Walsh, a critic and poet, is chiefly remembered as the friend and correspondent of Alexander Pope – Pope held him in very high esteem. Walsh was also a friend of John Dryden.

### WALT WHITMAN (1819–1892)

Whitman is one of the most influential of American writers, and his work was part of the transition from Transcendentalism to Realism in nineteenth-century American literature. His collection of poems *Leaves of Grass* did not immediately find favour among critics, but Whitman was not discouraged and continued revising the book throughout his life, bringing out a final 'deathbed edition' in 1892.

### OSCAR WILDE (1854–1900)

Oscar Wilde's reputation as a writer and key figure of the Aesthetic movement of the late nineteenth century is now inextricably bound up with his homosexuality. He was sentenced to two years in prison for homosexual offences and after his release went into exile in France. He died in Paris from cerebral meningitis.

### JOHN WILMOT, EARL OF ROCHESTER (1647–1680)

Rochester is as famous for his dissolute lifestyle as for his poetry. He was a courtier at Charles II's court, which had turned its back on the Puritan era. As befitted a poet of the Restoration, he was witty, rakish and often immoral. Not surprisingly, his poetry fell out of favour during Victorian times but has enjoyed renewed interest since.

*Love Poetry*

## GEORGE WITHER (1588–1667)

Wither was a poet, pamphleteer and satirist, and his more controversial writings landed him in prison on more than one occasion. He supported the Parliamentarian cause during the English Civil War, fighting under Oliver Cromwell, but later devoted most of his energies to his own legal proceedings in a bid to recover what he had lost when his home had been plundered during the war.

## WILLIAM WORDSWORTH (1770–1850)

Wordsworth was instrumental in launching the Romantic movement in English literature, and *Lyrical Ballads*, which he published together with Samuel Taylor Coleridge, was a kind of manifesto for the movement. From now on poets could express themselves in 'the real language of men' rather than in the poetic diction of the eighteenth century. Wordsworth was Poet Laureate from 1843 until his death in 1850.

## SIR HENRY WOTTON (1568–1639)

Wotton was a diplomat, politician, poet and courtier of James I. He was clearly held in very high regard, both as a writer and as a statesman, but his poetry remained unpublished during his lifetime.

## SIR THOMAS WYATT (1503–1542)

The Renaissance poet and diplomat Sir Thomas Wyatt is considered the father of the English sonnet; his foreign missions exposed him to classical and Italian styles of poetry – including the sonnet – which he then adapted for his own use and introduced to English audiences. He was rumoured to be Anne Boleyn's lover and was imprisoned in the Tower of London on a charge of adultery. He was freed only once she had been executed.

## ELINOR WYLIE (1885–1928)

Wylie, an American poet and novelist, enjoyed great popularity in her lifetime but never quite achieved the posthumous fame that might have followed. She had an unhappy childhood, and as an adult was known for her tortured love life – she had many affairs and married three times. She died of a stroke at the age of forty-three.

## W. B. YEATS (1865–1939)

William Butler Yeats was part of the Protestant Anglo-Irish minority in Ireland, but his Irish roots were critical to his identity and to his work. He was heavily involved in the Celtic Revival, a movement which advocated a turning away from English influences and a return to Celtic traditions and culture. He was awarded the Nobel Prize in Literature in 1923.

*Love Poetry*

# Index of Poets

# Index of Poem Titles

*Love Poetry*

# Index of First Lines

By this he knew she wept with waking eyes 242

My sweetest Lesbia, let us live and love 20
My true love hath my heart and I have his 29

Never give all the heart, for love 285
Never seek to tell thy love 146
Never shall a young man 281
No one so much as you 249
None ever was in love with me but grief 238
Not marble nor the gilded monuments 41
Now sleeps the crimson petal, now the white 212
Now the lusty spring is seen 64
Now thou has loved me one whole day 70

O my Luve's like a red, red rose 125
O! never say that I was false of heart 45
O Rose thou art sick 146
O thou, my lovely boy, who in thy power 47
O yonge fresshe folkes, he or she 26
Oh! Death will find me, long before I tire 247
Oh what can ail thee, knight-at-arms 134
Oh, when I was in love with you 277
One day I wrote her name upon the strand 34
One that is ever kind said yesterday 280
Out of the rolling ocean the crowd came a drop
    gently to me 207

Passing stranger! you do not know 209
Phyllis is my only joy 118
Pious Selinda goes to prayers 121
Prais'd be Diana's fair and harmless light 58

Red lips are not so red 251

*Love Poetry*

332                                           Love Poetry

*Love Poetry*